T0103839

THE GRAINS OF POTENTIALS

FESTUS O CHUKWUMA

THE GRAINS OF POTENTIALS

FESTUS O CHUKWUMA

PARTRIDGE

THE GRAINS OF POTENTIALS

Copyright@2016 by

FESTUS O CHUKWUMA

Ist Published June 2016

ISBN-Softcover- 978-1-4828-5873-0

ISBN-ebook- 978-1-4828-5874-7

Published by

PARTRIDGE INDIA

Print information available on the last page.

To ORDER Additional Copy of this BOOK Contact.

PARTRIDGE INDIA
PHONE/CONTACT NO: 000 800 10062 62
EMAIL: orders.india@partridgepublishing.com
WEBSITE: www.partridgepublishing.com/india

Contents

INTRODUCTION

Every human, irrespective of colour, location, age, Educational level or Background has immense potentials lying within them waiting to be explored. Some have got many or more than others, why some have only one. But it depend on how we explore the very little within us. Like the parable Jesus told his disciples about the Master and his servants. He said; one of the servants was given five talents, why the second was given two talents and the other one talent. He admonished them to trade with their various talents. This is applicable to every one of us living on the surface of the earth, knowing that we are all here on a mission for our master. The maker of the universe, who has implanted in us various talents to actualize our individual destiny, we all have responsibility to cultivate these talents or seed grains lying within us and to multiple them.

However, for us to truly achieved that height of success. We must acknowledge the fact that we all have talents and are all gifted with sufficient grains of potentials that we definitely need to get to our destiny successfully. To really channel ourselves, we must begin to consider or look inwardly, beyond what people think of us. Our maker "God" have guaranteed us that we all have got talents giving by him and he said; all we needed have being given. All we needed is already available, we need to be aware of this gift and nurture it and make it grow to maturity where the world can see. Our gifts as human are different and could increase and grow, even multiply. But we need to discover these gifts by asking ourselves or looking inwardly; what gift do i have? What i am passionate about? What my mission on earth and how can i accomplish it? Who and what is needed to accomplish it?

Success is simply a satisfactory realisation of a given goal or task. Realisation of a set objective, but only effective utilization of our potential can take us to the realm where we can have that feeling of satisfaction. No matter the level of a man, if the feeling of contentment or satisfaction is not there he is yet to actualised destiny. Once satisfaction is not attainable, one is not yet at destiny.

Success is a universal desire, everyone yearn for success in one form or the other, unfortunately majority don't get at it; either they live a duplicate life or do the wrong thing different from their original potential, because they are trying to please or emulate people. To actualise your divine destiny you must be your real self and use that which God have deposited in you. Remember all a seed needed to grow to maturity is already deposited in the seed; you already have it all in you, just like a seed. There is no future, which has no root on the past and in the present.

THE GRAINS OF POTENTIALS

Many people chase the dreams of others; copy others, why others wallow in an endless search of their true purpose. Some go from place to place, from one job to another, from one career to another. At the end they blame one thing or another, or even blame people for their mismatch of purpose. Anything you are not passionate about, makes you a demon of murmuring, you complain at every bit of it while on it. Why go from one profession to another? from one job to another after being tired of another hoping to make fortune, at the end you still end up in frustration without actualisation or little achievement or even nothing to show for it. That is not destiny because you got no satisfaction.

Your life is a gift from God; you are beautifully and wonderfully made. You have got the image of God at work in you. You are a creator by destiny, an inventor by divine agenda, you are a god. A being with an immortal Spirit, you can do exceedingly all things through Christ that strengthen you. You have got the backing of the most sufficient God, the maker of the universe, you have an almighty father. The creator that was never created, you lack nothing. Look inwardly today and see your gift, think it out, nurture it and grow it to maturity. Did you still remember that after the creation of the world, God gave man dominion over everything? Friends, we are in charge, please take charge of your destiny.

Your success lies within you, how do i know? God said; after the creation, all was good 'including you and i'. If the one that is called the alpha and omega, the one that knows the beginning and the end, even before you begin, he said you are good. Meaning he already sees your end, even in your beginning. He already knows that you will have a good success that was why he said all was good. So why are you confusing yourself by copying others or following people because you want to be something you are not made to be. You are a unique individual with a divine agenda.

Without your realisation of your potential you can't dominate, no matter your level of Education, you will still have the fear that will always put you down even at the least of challenges. Realisation of your given potential is confident. When you are working on the part of divine purpose you are passionate and highly motivated. No child that don't know his name or will not answer to it when called. Potential is a seal attached to our lives we can't do away with it, it's a drive that propels us if we must live a victorious life.

We all have the same starting point; which is our birth, but do you ask yourself why others are more successful? Some are professionals in their field, why others are apprentice; some still are yet to initiate a direction. At birth our lives is like a seed grain planted, giving to us by God to cultivate and produce good fruit. All that a seed grain needs to grow to become a big plant is already deposited in the seed. A cashew seed can't produce a mango fruit. Though the seed has it all within it to grow into maturity and produce good fruits, yet it must produce it kind. But it depends heavily in some various factors, ranging from; the climate, environment, the seed authenticity, weather condition and so on. The same is applicable to man's potential.

My father was a great farmer, may his soul rest in perfect peace. We use to cultivate different crops. As a child, I was privilege to watch him closely during the planting and harvest seasons. Often times during the planting season, after the first rain and burning of the bushes. We prepare the soil for planting; my dad is good at mix cropping. Often times he admonish us to plant some crops before others, because a particular crop mature before the other or because of how resistive that particular crop is, in line with the climatic condition. Often we comply and the harvest is always awesome. Season after season we anchor on this instruction, just as the farm land produces different crops in same particular piece of land in mix cropping so are we humans. We are endowed with several potentials, but we must work on the most passionate once first. The journey of a thousand miles begins with a foot step. If we cultivate our most passionate potential, success is guarantee. We must acknowledge within us, what first and what follows.

So many people have chase success in a very odd way that had lead them to failure. Some have missed it, others have missed it and retrace their steps, believe me the nature of a grain or quality of a grain is a booster. If the grain is not planted in a well prepared soil or the climatic condition is not suitable, or probably if the grains are not guided or protected against weeds and pests it may end up producing a poor harvest. Just as the seed grains or the little crops are protected against weeds and pest, we need to guard our thoughts and destiny jealously. Void of being devoured, if we must absolutely harness our grains of potential.

There was a particular year when we waited for the early rain of the year (first rain), but it took a longer time to come. So we acted impatiently, there was a great resultant effect. When we planted our seed grains, the procedure of planting was not followed accordingly or in line with how resistant they where, just Like my dad admonish us to plant a particular crop before the other. Instead it was the other way round, when we were about planting the one we should had planted first. We have to remove the other once in strategy position where the first one could have being planted. And that lead us to uproot a lot of the other crops that was already planted even when they have started germinating. Imagine the once that was uprooted have lost out of the season.

So many people have missed destiny out of chasing the wrong thing first and they never retrace their steps, so they lost out completely. Some end up losing their lives, others being displaced because they could not identify or locate their purpose, some are at the wrong place at the right time. We must be very careful the way we go about things in life, mostly things that have to do with our life, purpose and thought, if we must actualise our purpose on earth. Our attitude and thought must absolutely be on check constantly and continuously. To succeed we must fully guard our thought to harness our God given potentials.

In the farm why many grains are planted; some germinate grow and produce good fruits, others grow and produce bad fruit, some never germinate. Why some germinate, but could not withstand the environmental hazards, so they fell off along the line before maturity. To achieve destiny as human, we must nurture our thought, withstand our challenges and cultivate our grains of potentials within us. If we do it purifying our minds and thought, persisting along our way in all odd, keeping our imagination and innovative ideas in a constant growth alongside, our potentials will yield for us a great result positively and our destiny will be so awesome.

THE GRAINS OF POTENTIALS

There are some listed criteria and human qualities that will be considered in the following chapters of this book that will assist us discover ourselves and to achieve the successful growth of our grains of potentials to the extent of accomplishment.

Chapter 1

SELF DISCOVERY

For a seed to germinate it must be eager to see sunlight;
Passion is the foundation for self discovery

To fully maximize your God given potentials you must discover your true self and passion. In the journey of life, once you recognise or discover your passion and area of strength, work on it with great enthusiasm; surely you will achieve your purpose in life. As a little boy that is always in company with his dad at every planting and harvest season, i discover something one day at the farm during the harvest season. They were crops in some particular area that produce better harvest than others. I could not hesitate to ask my father why it was so. He said they are at the right location and the soil in which they were planted was suitable and better for the crop, and that is why they produce better harvest. So, i asked; what could be done so others could produce better? Really, i love good yield. He answered; they need more nutrients to grow well and produced better harvest since the soil where they are planted is not that good enough. Then i said; dad you don't apply fertilizer i remember you told me you don't like fertilizer yield, their yield don't last much after harvest you said; they get spoiled so fast when at store, he replied.

As i begin to get older, i begin to further study the crops and realised that my dad had long discover it and he had long prefer to use better seeds in those special locations where the harvest will be predictably great. We all have things we are very good at, we have got some areas or a thing we are very good at. Just that many don't admit to it or take the bull by the thorn. They communise it because they are very good at it, so they took it for pleasure. Most people hardly believe what they are good at could get them money or fortune, some will only calls it their hobby. Some will say i do it for fun; it's really not my job or business. Yet they spend most of their time doing it.

On like my dad that realised those special areas and plant better seed grains on it, and always getting good harvest at the end of the farming season. So many people have got potential that can take them to the pick of their field of endeavour. Though some saw it yet never believed or knew how to cultivate it as their divine purpose, so they lose sight of it. Why some never discovered it, because they were busy copying others. Some their guardian has mislead them into doing the wrong thing they never have passion for or studying the wrong course.

The easiest way to discover yourself; is to reflect on the things that you are passionate about as a child, when you where growing; like at the age of 7 to 14 years. Look inward of yourself they are things you do at ease and you gain huge success each time you do it. People often appreciate your effort and success at it anytime you do them. There is this thing you love to do naturally, why look down on it. Why allow your instinct to deceive you about it. That is your purpose, just work in that direction and seek ways to improve yourself at doing those things. No man on earth has always being a failure in everything, no matter how unlucky he or she is. You must have had success in one or two areas previously since your birth. All you need, it's to reflect on those areas and concentrate at doing them and do them better.

The moment you discover your passion and followed it, you begin to enjoy a smooth ride in your endeavour. No matter how little the seed look like, once the grain is planted on a good soil, it will definitely produce good harvest. Nurture your God given talent once you discover it at a very tender stage in life. Follow it, at first you may not know what will be at the end, but God knows already it will be good at the end. There may be some challenges along the way but the end is much rewarding than the pains you will experience.

I realised something one day, by packing seed grains on my pam. I discover that all the grains are not the same shapes nor are they the same sizes, even when they are same species yet they have their various unique nature or individuality. Just as the grains don't have the same shape or size, so are we. We all have our uniqueness and some specialty; we could be of same family or community or even same country but that little different is always there and that matters a lot, when it come to our personality or talents. Just as this little difference matters, so our potential differs and matters in the areas of our mission to accomplish on earth.

No man on earth is useless, except he never found his purpose. But we all are on earth on a mission and have come to accomplish a definite purpose. The joy of this our mission is that; all we need to accomplish this purpose is within us. The potentials are lying there waiting to be manifested. Is very important we discover these grains of potentials and work on them, no matter what challenge we face on earth they are all part of our journey to accomplishment. Some people pass through a lot before they discover themselves; some get along easier than others. But no matter how the journey looks, you must believe in yourself and always remember, the beginning of anything is not always easy. There is nothing like a prepared mind. To discover our selves we need to understand that the only different in people is the mind. The way we think varies from one person to another. Our environment, experience, present situation, background affects our sense of reasoning. But its better we purify our thought against negativity and other things that can prevent us from thinking right. The greatest strength of a man lies on his thought. A man is a product of his thought. How we think is what makes us unique.

One has to be connected to himself. Getting to know you and what you have got in your inside. It is so unfortunate that a lot of people are often connected to social media and friends more than themselves; as a result they get so many mixed up opinion and wrong guides. You are here to use your God given talents to better your world. Until you discover it nothing gets better. Not even your relationship with friends or the so called internet crazy stuffs of the present day can aid you destiny. You must discover yourself to be mastery at anything, it is so important in the journey of destiny. You got your grains of potentials waiting for you to acknowledge them and make effective use of them. Look on your inside; discover what you are passionate about, not what people wish you to be or what your guardians want you to be for them. Be that which God have given you unbeatable ability to accomplish, that will bring you satisfaction. Life is all about satisfactory living.

As a child i observed something during the harvest season in our farm that some crops produce better fruits than others. I didn't hesitate to ask my dad why it was so. He said they are at the right location and the soil there is better. With his answer in mind, i set to observe continuously all through the season what he told me. I was more curious why it was so and monitors him during the planting season since he already knows the better side in the farm yard. I found a great different as the year goes by; i notice he select special seed grains for those areas that seem better. One day i told him what i observed of him, and asked why we don't look for a way to improve the yield in those areas that are not such good. He reminds me that he doesn't like fertilizer application because the harvest don't last much when in store.

As i get older, i found out that same is applicable to human, when men are not found in the right profession or endeavour where their talent are fully utilized, they don't do well; they don't produce like those that are more motivated by what they do. Everybody have got great talent inside of him, we all have areas where we can be very good.

But because many live a life of copy and emulation, they don't discover themselves, some due to parents or guardian influence. Do you know when you do things that you are gifted to do; you don't get frustrated at doing it? No matter the challenge you encounter on your way. Because life is full of challenges, is advisable you do what you are passionate about, not what your parent want you to do or what you see your friends doing. Believe me nobody will ever help you to fight life challenges that you are not prepared to confront.

The advantage of doing what you love is that; you will be happy doing it, you will get satisfaction at it, you don't get frustrated at it no matter the challenges, you always have a solution when confronted with a tough situation. The fact that you love what you do, growth is definitely accessible and nearby. Though it is assume that before one becomes mastery in a particular thing, he or she must have done it over ten thousand times, but if you are not motivated you can't preserver for such long. There is no joy in murmuring, you will have to murmur many times and with continuous complaining when you are in the wrong profession or career. In our today world so many live all their lives complaining about what they do or about everything around them, just because they fail to discover what they are passionate about.

Self discovery is a sure step to success and actualisation of destiny. There are two most important days in a man's life, the day he was born and the day he discovers his true purpose on earth. Life without purpose is doom. Life has always reviewed our potentials at one stage of our life or another, because God is faithful; these talents are mostly review at the early stage of our life. Nobody that has gotten to age eighteen without at one point or another came across their God's given talents. But sometimes one could be so naive to observe it. Sometimes our guardians help us to discover it, and encourage us. But so many parents don't even observe their kids to see these things in the children and they help to frustrate the child the more by forcing their kids against the will and purpose of God.

If you could not fellow up with your God given talent early enough, it is not still late you can retrace your step and start again. No experience in life is waste, even the experience you gain at doing the wrong thing is useful, but better you discover yourself earlier in life. Never be discouraged or depress that you can't get it right again. You must stand up from where you are; if you can look up, you can get up and get started again. Every height is attainable with the required skills, just as every skill is learnable, what matter most is for one to discover what he is passionate about. But before you can be positive about life, you must forgive yourself and everyone else that could have not seen those things in you to help you get on it earlier enough.

Life is all about passion, because a lot of things pose as challenges to us, so once you not motivated on your inside you can't do well in that field. Today we have got so much distractions ranging from family influence on us, friends and environment. Even the social network of today is a big trait, though it is a good source of information, it also a great time killer and distraction. Believe me, some information people get online will never help them to discover themselves. It can completely endanger their creativity and self discovery, at the end results to a great time wastage and distraction from the things you ought to do. It is high time people sit up and start looking on their inside.

A boy was admonished by his father that he "talks too much". Because each time he goes out with the dad he asks questions about almost everything they come across. To the extent that he even interrogate his dad's friends with lots of questions. Often times his dad's friends get embarrassed of his questions. He had often provoked his dad with his attitude of always asking questions. His father decides he will not take him out again. The little boy so much likes to go out with his dad. As a daddy's boy, he pleaded with his dad several times. So, the father has to make a deal with him that he will be quiet or never ask any question whenever he takes him out, the boy accepted.

But one day they went out for a conference and he saw press men and women asking dignitaries questions, the little boy stopped and begin to watch them. The father observed him and asked him to come forward; he ran to his father and pleads him and said; "take me to those people" the little boy pointed at them. His father asked; what for? So you can begin your usual character of asking questions. The little boy said no, he only want to know why those people they are asking questions are not provoked, even some are telling them thank you. But people don't tell me thank you, the boy said; even your friends feel embarrassed when i asked them questions, they always get angry at me. That is why i want to know how those men are asking their questions. So people can be telling me thank you also.

The father told him, you must go through their kind of training before you can be like them, only then people can appreciate you when you ask them question and get your 'thank you'. First you need to get into high school, get the required papers and go into college to study related course like mass communication, Journalism etcetera. Before you can be qualify to do their kind of job. The boy was lucky enough to have a dad that understood his passion and encouraged him toward his purpose. Immediately the boy told his dad, "that what i want to become when i grow up". So they went into the conference hall and after that day. The boy kept on disturbing the dad regarding the training and what he needs to do to get it fast. The dad starts encouraging him on his studies and told him the necessary course he must pass to get into the university.

The boy read his life out in order to make those papers and finally got into the university to study mass communication. With the view that he will become a journalist and be qualify to ask anybody question irrespective of who the person is, he ensure he studied hard. Went through all the huddles and made it to his finals. After graduation, some months later he got a job with one national television station and step into his dream.

Two years into the job he won best script Editor. Some years after, he began to anchor news and was very passionate about his job. Awards after award begin to roll in and he became so famous and one of the most famous News caster of his time and an award winning journalist.

This is the benefit of doing something you are passionate about; you never get tired of it. The little boy discovered himself early enough. With the help of the father, he was immediately directed to what he has to do. Though most people have had such an in built ability, to discover their purpose or show such enthusiasm. Why some have nobody to direct their focus to the ladder, or to climb it. So they wallow in the dark of miserable search of their purpose. It is good when you have such people that understands or saw such ability in you earlier enough.

But if you don't, it's not still late to retrace your step and get it right. It is good to have a mentor or guardian that understand, but in case you got no one, cultivate the habit of reading and listen to materials that will build you up, motivates you and will help you discover yourself. So many people have parents that are Educated and understood the gift of their kids. Some people got mentors or someone mentoring them, it also very good. But the danger of mentoring is that some mentors enslave you or use you to achieve their own desire for wealth. But if you are lucky enough to meet good mentors that will help you grow is very good. But if you didn't, Reading materials from authors you admire can be a very good way of mentoring also and can help you to discover yourself. The character of a writer is always expressed in their write up.

If you not privileged to any of this; maybe you have tried a lot of things in life yet to discover your purpose? Spend time in reflection and meditation, with open heart you can get back to your child hood attitude and start over again. People that never discover themselves are those that see the world on their head or the world against them, they are full of negativity. They think they are the worst and can never make it again. But once you can think and live like a child again, you can get it right again. Be a child in the mind, have the brain of a mature person. What i meant is; stay away from jealousy, envy, bitterness, hatred and every negative memory of the past. Only in that way you can have the mind to think freely and discover yourself again and the grains of potential in you can be activated, cultivated and well nurtured till maturity.

To live a fulfil life; you must discover your purpose of existence. And believe me everybody is created for a purpose. You either have found your purpose before reading this book or not. You have got a purpose of being on earth. You got a calling, something you are uniquely created to do, something you should be very good at. Until you discover that thing you can't be absolutely satisfy, no matter your placement in the society. A lot of people have done things they never get satisfaction from. Some end up emulating other, at last they end up pleasing others by reaching their wish for them. You must understand your uniqueness, as one special entity living on the surface of the earth. You need to have self value to discover yourself.

The mind is the only thing that differentiates every human, how we think and the way we respond to things and challenges differs from one person to another. How we think and persistence ability in our various fields of endeavour goes a long way to discover if we have got a calling in that which we do.

Because if it's your calling or purpose you will never quit doing it, your enthusiasm for it will be high, you be resistance to challenges no matter how big or small. You will love it and be willing to do it over and over again; you dream it and it become part of your life to the extent that people see it in you. Purpose is not hidden. It's always significant only that a lot of people ignore it or take it for granted; they chase other things because they want to please people. Let's consider those attributes and attitudes that can help us discover ourselves, so we can fully utilize our grains of potentials.

SELF CONCEPT

Concept in life differ from one person to another, there is no two person's that see things in the same way. Self concept is a particular way someone see things. Our thoughts differ as human, so concept varies from one person to another. In various endeavour when challenges set in, some people see failure and could not continue, why another could see success in disguises. The one that saw failure will never be motivated no matter the resources at his disposal to accomplish his aim. But the one that already saw success must thrive to accomplish his aim no matter how scares the resources available for him to accomplish his aim. That is how self concept appears to everyone and it empower oneself to accomplish purpose. When you are at purpose all you see in your challenges is success or victory. Challenges don't really move you when you are on your divine purpose. Because you are motivated from your inside and never will you quit.

Once your concept about a thing, career, job or profession is wrong you can't do well at it. It is advisable not to even venture it, no matter how pushy people around you are. Stop and reflect and acknowledge is not your purpose. In your divine purpose you must have joy, enthusiasm and purpose driven.

Concept affects our reasoning, our appearance, our actions, our attitude, our ideal interest, our self esteem, and our relationship with others, even our confident about life. Purpose is relative to concept and it affects life positively or negatively pending on your calling and your attitude. It is always premonition about the issues of life which affects everything in our life and how we drive our purpose in life. Our potentials can either be active or not, pending on how we see things and our connection with humanity and purpose.

A lady that was supposes to use her gifts to serve God as her calling and purpose in life. Was molested and raped by a clergy man at her teens. She developed absolute hatred for anything like serving God. She lives with this guilt, and even until her adult age. This concept that the clergies are nothing to go by was implanted by one selfish man, and that placed the lady in absolutely miserable life style, to the extent that she became a prostitute and believes she is not good for any man. Imagine the innocent little girl she was when the ugly act was done to her.

Until she escape death, she could not forgive herself, even could not go to church again from the day of that incident. She just decides to live a wild life because of her early experience in life. She escaped death one day in the hands of ritualise, that intend to patronize her as a prostitute, she made a turn to God. When they took her to the place for ritual, in her shock she shouts; "Jesus"! The one to administer her for ritual request they should take her away. That was how God delivered her. In that shock and thought of how he name of Jesus delivered her, she got back her real self and gave her life to God and began again to walk in her purpose in life. Her concept about clergy almost destroys her life and made her life miserable for years.

Sometimes our experience builds our concept weather positive or negative, even when it may not be absolutely true. Like the lady concept about clergy. Really they could be bad once among them, but still i believe the number of the good ones out way the bad. But from her experience she never believes there could be a better one, since the one that suppose to be her school teacher slept with her in a molested manner.

Some people have made a superstition out from their experience, concept and believe, which is still affecting them until this day. One of the most harmful things about concept is superstition; believes that are imposed by fear of unknown, they are often registered in our subconscious mind. Some believe when they see a black cat on their way that the journey will be a bad one, even when it's not absolutely true. They forgot that anything you serve your subconscious mind is what it registers. And it becomes applicable to your action, motivation and will power, which at long reproduce it to either success or failure. A man is what his conscience made him; it is very difficult for someone that has conceived failure in his subconscious mind to be victorious. Take life bit by bit, make failure a friend and always bear in mind that true friends are not harmful; Failure can't lordly over you if it's your friend. If you are afraid of failure it will torment you never to venture, and you will always be subject to it (failure). If you must be successful in life you must nurse success in your heart, speak it, think it and dream it; that will propel you to achieve it.

Self concept determines your level of effectiveness in life or what you do with your life. How you perform and what you become greatly depends on concept about life. And what you become in life either good or bad is largely determine by your concept. It is your purpose if it brings you Joy and satisfaction, else it's not. An average person spends ten percent (10%) of their time in their productive endeavour or on their growth area daily. Why most of their time is spent on unproductive thinking, some mostly conceive only negative thoughts all day long; either how to hurt others or how others have hurt them. So many people use most of their early morning strength and ability to wallow on regret or pain of yesterday even before they leave their bed every morning. This is one of the major reasons why so many don't discover themselves. If the foundation be destroy what will the righteous do? I recommend that every reader of this book begin to work on their thought and their concept towards positivity, mostly at the early morning of everyday.

It so necessary to think more of the solution to that thing that appears like a challenge instead of the challenge itself. I encourage you to use only five percent (5%) of your time to think on the challenge the very moment you notice it, then after spend ninety five percent (95%) of your total time on possible solution until you accomplish it. When you make it a habit you will begin to win naturally. So many people find it difficult to forgive themselves, more of forgiving others. You must make forgiveness a habit, that the only way to do away with negative imagination. Forgive yourself, and forgive others. Your concept about that issue or situation will determine whether you make it bondage or a stepping stone.

Concept even affects eating habit of some people, even their type of friends. Some being so religious by nature love only those in their denomination; if you are not a worshipper of their church they hate you. They can as well assume you are not a good person. Can't you see that such a reason or concept can limit you in every level; why will you in your right sense put yourself in an everlasting bondage? Even Jesus Christ preaches the kingdom of God not religion. Your concept must be positive in all extent if you must get to your purpose in life.

A young man who has a great affection for a lady at her twenties, but her problem is that the young man is not her church member or same church and so she can't love the young man. Without even enquiring from God if he is her husband or not. Today at her late forty she is still single. Her Concept has destroyed her youthful age and kept her miserable. Some people are so race conscious, that they might have nothing to do with people of different language, culture or colour, even when they need help they will never ask because of their concept. Everybody must learn to see each other as one body in Christ, accept one another the way they are. The world is one village with many family of immeasurable uniqueness. It is wisdom to be much aware with the teaching of Jesus Christ, which is the kingdom of God.

Concept reflects through ways like dressing, expression and actions. Concept is a key to self discover and it is necessary to make it positive by every means possible. Let it be acceptable by majority to enable you more room to actually size up properly in the modern society. Self concept affects our relationship with people, family and friends. Even the way we spend money and what we spend our resource on is determine by our concept. So to discover your potential or purpose in life you must streamline your concept to the positive.

IDEAL TECHNIQUE

Our opinion and Idea inspire our value and concept, even our hope and dreams. Idea about anything is of great important if you must be mastery. An idea gives birth to creativity and innovation, without it growth will be least visible. For us to discover our true potential, we must have adequate idea or incite on the very field or endeavour. Anything you are gifted to do, as your God giving potential there must be sufficient idea to carry it on. Though sometimes it is required of us to learn and acquire adequate knowledge, but still your ideas no matter how little could be needed. Passion is not always enough without idea or incite. From the story of the little boy we read earlier on, the boy was passionate but he got no idea on how to ask people question without getting them embarrassed or angry. That was the reason why the father suggests he undergo the required training, go through college, graduate to become a journalist.

Imagine a banker on a faithful day; as he was about to start his car to zoom to his office, discovers his car battery went bad. No matter how passionate he is to fix the car, he needed an electrician to fix it. Else he will try it all day without fixing it. Idea is very essential, passion or enthusiasm is not always enough without idea. Remember what lies behind us or around us is a tiny matter compare to what lies within us. An idea can change your life; it is a key element to self discovery. As a man think in his heart so he is and nothing is more original to a man than his idea.

Have you ever ask why so many people pass through a lot before they arrive at destiny? I guess is because they have insufficient idea of which way to go or how to get their purpose going. So for them to discover who they really are and work towards it, they need ideas and skills required in that particular field to achieve their destiny. So all of the process where inclusive of training and is very necessary. It is very important that we channel our ideas, because it positions us to discover our grains of potentials and fully utilize them for our benefits and the benefits of others.

PASSION

Passion is a propeller to self discovery. If you must discover your gifts you must concentrate on the key areas of your passion, which will drive you to destiny. Without passion no one can really get to destiny. It is a key ingredient to achieving any desire. Whatever a man is passionate about, he has the tendency to actualise. This willpower called passion, makes your believe wax stronger and place your hope on; that you are going to accomplish that which you have set your mind on. It is the zeal to do a particular thing, the energy that set you apart for accomplishment.

A man with a great passion for business only needs little knowledge and support, but he without the passion will not even be willing to acquire the necessary knowledge.

Give a man without passion for studies the best library and the best facilities for learning he will still end up a failure. But if a man with passion is given the least of support he will definitely come out with flying colours. Passion is always the first runner, before training and support. Without it no matter the amount of support the aims will not be achievable. To discover you, you must look into that area you are truly passionate about, and passion will drives you towards it and guarantees your accomplishment.

SELF IMAGE

Our image is the reflection of our inner man through our character and composition. What you can see is the much you can become, if you can picture your future, lay hold on the image of the picture of the future you see and mobilize all resource at your reach to accomplish it. If what you see or what people see in you doesn't look like what you want of yourself, then you need to work on those odd things to conform to your calling and purpose if you must fully utilize your grains of potentials.

Concept plays a major role in building your image. A lawyer has a way of conduct, even dress code. Else people will question his image and character. So anyone with the passion for rules and law must conform to the image of a lawyer to discover his full potential for it. If you have to discover yourself and walk along with it to destiny you must conduct yourself image to suit that which you must become. It is very important you create a good image in line with that which you want to become or your potential once discovered; even your conduct can help people to predict your potential or purpose. Your image is the mirror reflection of you in play, which is what interacts with people; it should be jealously guarded. It helps your concept and believes to come alive, which aid you to self discovery. If you must discover yourself you must work hard to create a good image of yourself in order to discover your true potential and purpose.

SELF ESTEEM

Self esteem is the sharpener of destiny and propeller of purpose. It helps one build a character that enables him a smooth ride to discover destiny. It is call self regard and acknowledgement of one self, it help you to go through life with understanding of who you are. Walking in the consciousness of who you are and what you want to become, pave way for full utilization of your grains of potentials. It is necessary you learn how to appreciate yourself and others too. But if you don't have self esteem, you will definitely not know your purpose and may end up with undefined purpose.

A prince at the age of 4 years was left at home with his father's maids and guards, why his parents went on a journey. Because the little boy never knew who he was, the maids in the house where sending him errand. Because he never knew he was a prince or what is expected of a prince in the palace. So it is like one without self esteem, when you lose yourself esteem you may never notice and you can as well lose your identity. No one looses his/her self esteem without losing his identity. Self esteem is very important in the quest to discover ones purpose. There is no self benefit that is as great as appreciating who we are; your respect for self will determine your respect for others. If you don't love yourself the way you are, you can't pretend to love others. You only regard and appreciate others, if you truly appreciate yourself. You will not have a good self esteem without self appreciation; neither will you know how to appreciate others. Self esteem determines your discipline, composure and focus in life. To discover yourself you must build your esteem to suit your ideas, values and concept. The way you carry yourself, determines the way you think and your thought determine how far you can go in life. To discover yourself and fully utilised your grains of potentials you must have self esteem as a necessity.

Chapter 2

LOOSE YOURSELF
AND BE REFORM

Every seed decay to gain root and become a great tree;
to live in your dreams, you have to become the
person of your dreams

Seeds lose themselves to become plant. The eagerness of the seed to see sunlight leads it to germinate. If any seed want to germinate first it must be ready to lose itself. Lose it old nature of seed to become a tree or a plant. This process must be done for the seed to successfully gain root into the soil and enable effect growth.

Just as seeds so are our potentials, for you to discover yourself and achieve your destiny it's necessary to lose yourself. Before you made the decision to chase your dreams, you must already have a life you where living either good or bad. To drop that old life style aside for your purposeful life you have to lose yourself. To become something new you must walk in the image of the picture of that newness. People changes but change can only be effective by losing your old self. Something must be altered to experience change; it can't be business as usual. You have to be ready to drop some old characters and be willing to acquire new once. To be successful, you have to think and work like one and able to see success in challenges. To be rich, you have to dream and think like the rich. To be a king, you have to live like one. Anything you want different from what you are, you have to acquire the character necessary to match its demands. If you want to be a CEO you must act and think like a CEO?

It is necessary as part of your responsibility to acquire change, change don't just come, it is deliberate. Put off your old self or image to acquire the image of the person you want to become. To be victorious in life you must speak like victorious people, confess victory with confident and strategize effectively. You can't be thinking negatively and expect a positive outcome. To be positive you have to put away negative thoughts. To be productive you have to work harder and smart. Lazy men don't expect victory in life, no matter how talented you are you must train yourself. Practice and diligence makes one consistent and victorious.

Losing yourself takes process, and those processes are in stages, you are to love every part of the journey in the process to discover your grains of potentials. Beware murmuring and complaining is a distraction to this process. Sometimes losing yourself can lead you to losing friends, Losing yourself can lead you to relocating or even change of career or occupation. This why most people don't like the process they only want the end result. Everyone wants to be a star, but they forgot that stars shine alone. To shine like the sun you must be willing to burn like one. It takes dedication and diligent to keep keeping on. Focus and concentration is not always without distractions and challenges, its only being able to overcome them. Muscles don't make you a man, purpose driven ideas, perseverance and discipline makes you a better man.

Man needs challenges to enjoy victory; how do i mean? I mean before you can enjoy success you have to endure pains and difficulties. Let use this example to elaborate further; A case of two men, Mr A and Mr B. Mr A inherit wealth and living in affluence, enjoying every good thing of life, lives in Air condition apartment, home and car. He never experiences any form of difficulty or challenges as relate to money, he has it all working for him. Then he got carried away and he mismanaged his resources. His father's friend gave him opportunity to work in his office.

After some months he begins to regret his situation and how he lost his money. While Mr B had never known wealth, was poor Road side Mechanic at the street. One day favour locates him through a rich man who forgot his briefcase at his shop. The man gave him a better job and he began to enjoy the good things of life. The joy of Mr B knows no boundary because he had faced a lot of difficulties. He feel better at his new life because of the pain of his past, same favour was given to Mr A yet he felt no better, because he was wealthy before, and used to such life. Joy to me is the invoking of emotion that brings satisfaction, appreciation and pleasure. To be appreciative your present life should be better than your past. To have the pleasure and satisfaction your victory should be far beyond your pains and difficulties.

As a little child i had one experience to create more understanding to this view. Then still in high school, few miles away from home and i usually trek home after school whether rain or sun, climate is not a problem. When it is sunny and tense i often branch off to get some cold water from a sister's shop, did you know i enjoy the cold water when the sun is very high than when there is no sun shine. Sometimes i forgot to branch, even to say hello to my sister when it's raining, because she admonish me to always wait after the rain before going. I enjoy resting at her shop when it's sunny, because it cools the heat within me and enable me to enjoy the cold water. Such is applicable to success. The stress and the pain make the celebration of success worthwhile.

No matter how tall your father is, you have your own growth to make. You need to feed well to grow well. "If you refuse to grow, people can only see you as the son of that tall man". If you are dwarf you make your existence miserable because even your father will deny if you are his true biological son. Even why lions don't give birth to goat, the baby lion must learn to hunt for himself in the jungle if he wants to survive.

Growth in life is personal, just as its personal for every child to grow, no matter how tall their parents are. No matter how adventurous your parents were, you need to venture with your own drive and ideas to be outstanding. Nobody lives for anybody no matter the legacy left behind. Great achievements is not hereditary, because they are acknowledge with affluence not only wealth. You can inherit the wealth but not the affluence; you must pass through your own process, discover yourself, lose yourself and work on your potentials to become successful and influential.

Except a seed fall down and dies, it does not produce a better seed. No matter how big a yam seed is, if it must produce tuber, it must be ready to germinate and decay. In life you must lose yourself to fine your true purpose. If everything is working your way it will be very difficult to discover yourself. Any object on motion opposes gravity; don't let that challenge that acts as gravity to keep you back. You must come out of your comfort zone to initial a move and make a stand. Rest or comfort is good but is not always helpful to discover your grains of potential. Stones are of same component with soil, but before a stone can become a soil, it must be mesh or grinded into small pieces to form a soil.

Challenges make you grinded and prepared you to chase your dreams. Don't shy away from challenges, face it and let it make you. Seeds don't gain root except they decay, and they can't stand except they have root, the stronger and deeper their roots, the taller and thicker their stems and branches. Lose yourself to discover your grains of potential and true purpose in life.

During decay or when you are in the valley of life, that when you truly discover yourself and who you truly are. If you can be positive in that miserable life, you will soon discover yourself and become successful. "Growth is best in the valley of life, because if you can grow at the valley you can always do better at the mountain top". It is easy to lose a silver spoon if it's given to you in the crowd, but very difficult to lose it if you made it yourself. Silver and gold spoon attracts more attention and challenges on like wooden spoon in the real sense of life, so be prepared to make them instead of acquiring them. Precious stones are not found on the surface of the earth. You have to dig deep to discover them. Give yourself room to think, to learn in order to discover your purpose and grains of potential. Losing yourself will be very helpful in gaining the required strength or root to withstand, let us consider some human behaviour and attitude that can enable one lose self.

DON'T EVER THINK YOU ARE SPECIAL

Only those that have achieved success and earn their affluence are treated specially. We all see this play out in the society we live in. Every society has the people that stir it, either through leadership, business, Education, health and utilities. A word changes my perception about feeling special one day. "God use ordinary things to humble the pride". It's good to influence people with your skills and personality, but don't be carried away by the affluence you receive. Anytime you know what to do and you did it humbly and sincerely heaven supports you. Lose that usual everybody feeling special attitude of many or want to feel special kind of life, just concentrate on the task and get it done. Make the task at hand your priority and with humility you will surely get it done.

You know when special feelings become harmful? Everybody with affluence have team. This team have being trusted over time and years, before they hit fame. So the fame that brought them affluence has being so challenged in different areas of their individual attitude and team spirit. But as someone on the process of self discovery, you must lose yourself, to fine your purpose. Humility is strength that can always open any door, when accompany with honesty it does magic. Humble yourself to discover your purpose. I realise one thing in life one day; did you know what i found out about life? No matter whom you think you are or what you feel you are, you don't own yourself. Someone owns you and decides what happens to you.

Though they are natural laws that declare instant judgement on man, but there is someone that decides. God decides everything, he is the maker of the universe even nature obey him. He loves humble people so much; he even promised to give them earth as their possession. He can give this whole earth to them as much as they remain faithful to him. To retain his sustenance is to remain humble to him, but he forces no one. It's wisdom and with great humility to always acknowledges God in everything.

Losing yourself is unleashing the feeling of supremacy, even when you assume a leadership position, God is still the leader. Then you can be at peace with your position and subjects, because God is the king of peace. If it requires a leader to be humble to access the incomparable grace of God. How much more you that is trying to get on track to discover your purpose. Life recognises only those that affect them. If you think you are special and not affecting lives you will have no recognition from life. Life is in everybody, the more people you affect, the more life recognises you. Self confident is a strong believes on one's ability, to believe yourself you have to be sure of your God and to be sure of your God you have to be obedient to him.

You have every reason to be humble, but you need to choose people also to listen to and be humble and loyal to them also. If they deserve your trust and loyalties give it and make them part of your life. No man is an Island, nobody knows it all, two good heads is better than one. Partnership is strength that gives Joy and reduces risk. Joy is invoked by the feeling of satisfaction, pleasure and appreciation. The more you appreciate your partner or friend the closer and better your relationship.

Assuming you are special can destroy your relationship with others; it can make you edged out. Have you ever had this thought, if everyone begins to feel special, then who will be loyal or humble. In such society nothing works, because they will be too proud to see challenges. A functional society is the one that deploy both human and natural resources to tackle challenges or problems. People that saw a problem and solve it are the people life recognises. No matter who you are, try to lose yourself to discover your divine purpose, because when you found yourself, nothing can ever stop you again.

Humble yourself so when you found yourself, you hold on to that picture of yourself. Every other thing will fall in place for you when you are walking on divine purpose. Life is all about finding your purpose for creation; successful people are those people that worked on their purpose. If you found your purpose hold on to it, and run with it. Until you find it nothing like affluence or special feeling, because only the successful are treated specially. Apart from people making you feel special, every other special feeling is pride.

LET GO OF YOUR WEAKNESS

I realise something from an experience; people hold on too long in their area of weakness. They try to make impression in something they are not good at, they aren't even motivated at it, yet they hold on to it. If you are weak at something the best you can become, with all the effort is average. The reason is clear; if you are not good at something you have no talent that motivate your action in doing it. So with all the effort and time invested you will only become average. This is a more reason why you need not hold on to your weakness. Everybody have something they are good at, or they can be good at. You have to concentrate on your gift. Train yourself more on it and soon you will be very good at it.

If you hold on to your weakness, you may delay your destiny or never found it. Imagine someone that can't sing, never on his own start singing or have any thought about music as intuition. Wake up one day and said he wants to become a musician. If you can't sing for yourself you can't sing for others. You can't become that which you can't see in you.

Training make you better, but anything you are gifted on you should be able to do it above average, even without training. That a proof of your gift and strength area. People must appreciate it, even when at its earlier stage. It must be seen in you. Talents are not hidden. Stop working on the areas where you are not gifted, rather work on your strength, that which others appreciate in you. Drop your weakness not because you can't improve if you try, but because you can't gain mastery and you're weak at it.

Talent is strength, work on your talented areas. The more training you give it the better it gets. It is important you know those things you do with the least of effort and yet get good result. Those things are part of you. Those things you do without too much error or correction. Those are the things you needed more effort to try and be better on. If your work on your strength area continuously, it enables you to stay focus with your purpose. Your purpose is you and you are what you make out of life. So be willing to work on your strength and let it defines you, because that is who you are.

Loosing yourself demands you let go of your weakness, don't ever believe that you can master everything. Even why you can do something's you may not be very good at it. Don't try to work on your weakness, when you have not found your true purpose. If you know is your weakness just acknowledge it and let go of it. Concentrate on your strength and give it your best, with it you will discover who you truly are and how your talent can affect others positively. Your sense of responsibility brings in the benefit and satisfaction that its success carries.

BE PASSIONATE AND SHOW COMPASSION

The enthusiasm, feeling or eagerness to accomplish a goal or task is passion. If you must achieve success your passion for that which you do must be high. When you lose yourself in your passion? That when you begin to act on your purpose unconsciously. It's simple indication that you are in to discover your destiny. Before every seeds begin to grow it must initially undergo a process called germination. Germination occurs out of the seed willingness to see sunlight. Same is applicable to man, for you to see success in anything you must be passion driven. Passion built confidence in a man. If you ever have a dream, let passion drives you; your confident will swing to actualization. A dream driven by passion, good decisions and discipline will one day be a success story. If there is a will there is a way. A man with passion will definitely get an opportunity to do that which he is passionate about some day. Passion doesn't recognise obstacles. Passion energizes positive thought and destroys doubt, that makes it so useful in the discovery of man's potentials.

If you are a compassionate person and you got passion for something? You are one of the best human species ever. A compassionate man with passion does extremely well in any endeavour. It's the best way to drive a goal, business or group. With passion at same time seeing things from your beloved point of view, from your customers point of view and from your colleague point of view. That broadens your understanding of the system. Your compassionate feelings for others enable you to see solution in their problem. Every problem has its solution around it. It takes passion to search for it and compassion to feel the problem even when it does not involve you.

One day two French Merchant traders went for a business in an Island. When they arrive at the Island, they where both surprise; one said, the citizens of this island don't even have shoes, they go about bal footed. This island must be lacking civilization gosh. Why the other man said there is business here, if one can just make shoes for the people of this island, guess they will buy. The first man was busy seeing the problem and magnifying it, explaining it even mocking them, soon he can begin to say their government is bad. Why the second man was compassionate about the people of the island and begins to reason ways to solve their problem. Most often compassion drives passion. Compassion can sustain you through challenges if you are passionate, with only appreciation until you achieve your goal.

After their trade, they both left. The first man went about his normal trade, why the second man went ahead to negotiate with a shoe maker and they made some rubber shoes to test the market on the island. Some weeks later he took the shoes to the island and he sold everything. Many that have no money to buy were exchanging their valuables with shoes and he made a great fortune. After some years the first man went back for a trade on the island and notices huge changes. The second man already an established factory owner in the island making shoes and everybody in the island where really looking nicely dressed. This is what compassion does to a man's destiny. It earns you love, resources and trust.

Compassion for others makes you lose yourself, but it energizes passion and gave birth to purpose. Once you have a purpose and you follow it, success is certain. An intelligent man creates something out of nothing, but a wise man makes use of something others reject. You can be intelligent and wise, but if you are compassionate with your passion you are in for a biggie.

Compassionate feelings humble the mind. It gives the sense of feeling for others. Most times one needs humility to see a solution in the problem of others. It's the easiest way for them to appreciate you or follow you, if you must lead or direct their affairs. If you can solve someone problem you become an idol to that person; he gives you money, he is happy for you and at the same time he has his satisfaction and happiness too.

Lose yourself; be humble enough to see beyond the society problem. There is problem everywhere, if you don't provide solution where will the solution come from? Though someone else could provide it, but why can't the solution come from you? Challenges can't end, only men with great ideas and passion to stand up against the dust the challenges threaten with, are needed. You are a solution source, until you work in such awareness you can't make an impact. Growth comes through involvement in a change process, without your involvement you can't succeed and with your involvement you can't fail. There is nothing to lose in trying to proffer a solution to a challenge. Define the challenges and initiate an organised and planned solution.

Compassion triggers positive imaginations that boost your thoughts for creativity. If you are passionate about anything, see how it can benefit others and make it your strong reason for accomplishing that task. Soon you will realise that you are as well benefiting from it. There is always inter-relationship in every human within the universe. There is that thing in you the world is waiting for, yet you don't believe you can. If you are passionate about it, try to picture yourself doing it, you can do it, go and do it, you will succeed.

ALWAYS BE CONTENTED

Contentment is the attitude of joyful and happy people. It's the attitude that gives you the sense of satisfaction before the actual satisfaction. It brings comfort and peace to a man's heart. Contentment makes you happy with yourself and achievements. If you are not happy for yourself you can't be happy for others, if you don't love your life nothing will interest you in life.

To discover yourself, you must acknowledge your existence as a privilege and be happy for being part of life. Only then you can decide to do something meaningful with your life. Most people conceive the thought of suicide every day, some have committed it and some want to do it now while other are still thinking if they can undergo such painful process. Let me tell you something you are not the worst person, only you want to show yourself as the cup bearer of murder, which you don't need.

First be happy for who you are now good or bad. Laugh about it, all your negative actions and failures. Make sure you laugh over them very well. Then take responsibility to do something to better your life every day, no matter your age now, if you do it consciously and continuously for years soon your life will be great. Contentment is the foundation for growth; it motivates and gives you a second chance to try again. You see things clearly if you are contented about what you got the clearer picture of where to consolidate your growth will be unveil.

The attitude of contentment creates the room for personal satisfaction, appreciation and happiness which has a great impact on personal development. If you can appreciate your present phase you can see the next phase. Life is phase by phase. Contentment creates the joy within individual that can guarantee constant growth with good decisions and discipline in the pursuit of purpose. Contented people see failure as a feedback, why others see failure as weakness. When failure becomes weakness nobody wins. But seeing failure as a feedback energises you to try again with greater expectations.

Contentment undoes the shame of defeat or failure. It gives you peace and opportunity to prepare better. No matter the challenges in life, if you have breath you can still win. Don't let challenges push you to inpatient or greed, you may lose focus. Instead you lose focus for greed and inpatient better you lose your greed and are contented. Our flesh can fight us most often when things don't go our way. But be contented, don't lose focus rather lose yourself, before you lose you. You lose you when you allow greed and inpatient to get hold on you, and then your flesh will begin to rule your mind. "Any seed that refuse to decay will not grow well". Allow something's to happen, don't be shameful for something that is gainful. Face your fears; there may never be a better opportunity to do it than now. The seed that lose itself is decaying to gain root and grow to become firm and produce better, but decaying stink; just as humiliation, shame and reproach stink to man. But in it all men discover themselves and their true purpose. Losing yourself through contentment even when your flesh opposes your decisions is a surest way to discover your true purpose.

Contentment creates the positive mindset that allows you to aim and achieve your purpose. It leads you humbly to your grains of potentials, because it helps you lose every negative thought. Contentment helps you to lose every negative wave that is capable of making you a mediocre. Negative thoughts like; bitterness, worries, fears and weakness etcetera. This negative thoughts or feelings are capable of destroying one's life or destiny. This is why is very important to be contented about life, because it gives you the satisfaction that keeps your dreams and focus alive until you achieve your goals. Be contented at all times to avoid those negative emotions that are capable of preventing you or your goals from seeing the light of the day. If you can continue to express satisfaction in life you will continue to shine.

SEE MONEY AS A RESPONSIBILITY NOT A REWARD

Responsibility means taking control or charge over something, functions or activities. Just as it works for human, so it is; when money becomes responsible it begin to create functions and activities that will enable it to wax on its subject. When money is a responsibility it solve problem and wax stronger. On the other hand, if money becomes a reward? It earns for every input. This expectation of pay package makes it very impossible for anyone that sees money as a reward to lose self.

When money is a responsibility you earn sufficient wisdom to direct and control both resources and man power through different stages of growth and development. A man, who saw a problem in the society and took responsibility to solve it, will have more money than the man who is hire to solve a problem in the society. The one that took the responsibility will think, analyst the problem and use men to solve it. On the other hand the man that is hired wants to be rewarded with pay package after his input. You earn wisdom out of taking responsibility, it only requires your ability to humble yourself and see the needs of the people, in the process of providing solution you learn and acquire skills, even master the process to provide such need in most sophisticated manner that will facilitates end result in more refined and better quality. Taking this kind of responsibility get money into the system for effect control and directing of both human and material resources.

You lose yourself, when all you do is to take responsibility of a situation; you acquire wisdom also in the process. Taking responsibility makes money flow in your direction, but the benefit don't start coming until the responsibility is fully taken. That makes it very impossible for an inpatient man. When you expect to be paid for everything, you be very unwilling to learn or take responsibility for anything that you will not earn from. Activities that do not attract instant reward will not be interested to you. You are the pay as you go kind of person. Your creative imaginations often times will not be effective. Instead of trying to learn new things or even create an avenue for training, you rather seek a short cut where you can just get rewarded with money.

In life not everything we do, we earn money from or expect money. Some things are to train us for the future challenges, most are to build us and make us better. Like a student going to school; it's only acquiring knowledge that will help withstand future challenges, knowledge that will still help him solve problems and give him confident to take responsibilities. It will take the student humility to gain impact, patient to acquire enough knowledge and become mature to undertake any task. Losing yourself requires you seeing money as a responsibility; meaning you see problem that you can solve before its benefit. Before you can benefit from taking a responsibility you need to deploy all your ability of imaginative thinking, planning and organising for effective delivery. It takes process to achieve success. Any success you don't earn wouldn't last. Everyone that achieved success learnt something in the process if the success deserving.

You lose yourself to pass through the required training necessary to grow your potentials in life. In the process; you learning, training, strategizing, organising and executing etcetera. All these stages require great attention and commitment. Success is not cheap; it requires humility, dedication and hard work. To grow you need to learn on a process, to learn you need to be humble and acquire all the required skills necessary to truly discover your grains of potentials.

CHAPTER 3

RESILIENT AND ADAPTATION

The deeper the root, the taller the tree.
The more the challenges the more opportunities for growth

For every plant to grow successfully and produce good harvest, it must produce root to help the plant withstand wind and other environmental challenges. Resilient is the ability to withstand challenges. It keeps you strong all through adversaries. It gives you ability to adapt to all conditions.

There is no field of life or endeavour that doesn't have its challenges. So your ability to resist and adapt will help to keep you going. You must be strong and focus in that area of your calling even after discovering your purpose you still need determination to resist constraints. Everybody in life at every point in time is either out of a challenge, facing a challenge or will soon face a challenge. No one is exempted from challenges in life. The great and successful see challenges as a stepping stone, why failures always wish they were never born when they meet challenges; they seek a way to avoid them. But when they can't found it, they quit. Why it is important to discover once purpose in life; it is also necessary to know that there will always be challenges before you get to your destination, in order to fulfil purpose.

As a little boy i realise something in the farm one day. After we planted our crop and they started growing; there are often heavy rains that blew great wind. During the raining season in the mangrove region of Africa and most often some plant falls, some bend and other might not even bend an inch. The once that fell will be uprooted and dispose, why we try to stand the once that bend. After which some yet may end up not making a good harvest as a result of those challenges. I remember my father instructing me to cut off the once that fell and dispose them, i ask him why can't we stand them like we did to the once bending? He said it's not necessary because they can't stand anymore.

In life, is necessary to be alert of life challenges. Prepare your mind and acknowledge in reality that it will always come someday. It is important to begin to build your strength against future challenges. The well rooted plants can always withstand the wind and most environmental hazards. Automatically the fallen plants are lost and never got to the harvest season. In a simple language their life and growth ended the day they were cut off.

Life challenges have cut so many people off, some are walking dead. They are bodily present and can't withstand their challenges so they quit. Some quit at the "someday island". At the very beginning of founding their purpose they quit. Some murmur through life and complain over everything. If you are in any of these category and you are reading this book you are not yet cut off from life. Only try to read this book to the end and work with the lay down principles to overcome those challenges that dread you in that area of your calling.

Believe me you have all it takes, only you have fail to work on them to produce for you a root to withstand or stand firm when those challenges surface. So many great destinies are in the grave today because they could not withstand life challenges; some have lost all hope because the storm took them unaware. We are going to consider some key things that will enable us to stand strong when this life challenges come. Just bear in mind that as many individuals are different so their challenges varies. But whatsoever be your challenge at any point in life don't ever quit or give up on your dreams. Always remain focus, 'no matter the wind keep standing', be a rock. Challenges are often a stepping stone if you never thought of quitting. They open you to new things and you gain knowledge through deeper thought when you overcome any challenge in life. So many attribute have enabled great men to succeed, just as a lot of negativity has weakened the minds of others that ended up as failures.

If you resist negative thought you will be productive and successful, because your strength will be in full capacity that will aid you to achieve your purpose in life. Let's consider some negative attitude you need to do away with to stand strong and resistant to all your life challenges;

SELF JUSTIFICATION

Don't always justify yourself whenever you face challenges in life. It destroys your ability to reason or seek a solution. Some people always see the cause of their failure or challenges in others; if you are in this category please stop it. Say this word whenever you face challenges "i am responsible" and try to laugh over it. Then take charge, wisdom and solution come to people that like to take responsibility of their situation. When you relate your challenge or failure to someone or something you are trying to justify yourself and your sense of reasoning will weakened towards seeking for a solution. And is a great sense of quitting.

Great minds don't seek ways to escape when they face challenges or blame people for it. Rather they face it with all their strength and might. Try to picture yourself as a root cause of your failure, only then the idea and solution to conquer will naturally come up from your thought. It could be to correct some character of yours or require you to bringing in some other persons into the boat to get your focus right again. So think solution than blaming others, it gives you sense of reasoning through and finding a lasting solution. Remember if you fine the solution once whenever you face such challenge again you already know how to win. But anytime you blame someone or something for your challenges you never get over it.

Another thing to note; it is important to take responsibility, but whenever you take responsibility don't spend too much time in blaming yourself or analysing the problem. So many people spend the early time of their day blaming themselves for their failure or thinking about their problem or challenges. You are advice to only spend five percent (5%) of your time on thinking about the challenge immediately it happened or occurred, why you spend ninety five percent (95%) of your time on seeking for the solution and thinking on the best way possible to solve the problem. We all may have held people; either family members or friends in our closest, apportioning blames and quarrelling most often. Those of us that grew in the villages experience this often. Some end up in fighting without even seeking for the solution to the problem, to some families the problem can even separate them.

It is far much better for you to spend most of your time in the early morning of the day thinking on the solution to that challenge or problem; be it academies, relationship, family or business challenge. If most of your thought and resources is channel towards seeking for solution soon you will found the solution, because everything you need to succeed in life is within you. So the solution is in you just that many people are not thinking on the solution. There is no challenge that you can't withstand that will ever come to you, always believe that. It will help to awaken your inner man. All your life challenges are surmountable if you take time to think on the solution instead of the challenge itself. Ask yourself these questions; what must i do? How can i do it? Can i handle it alone? Do i need to involve anyone? Who can proffer a solution or advice on it? With these questions going on in your mind repeatedly, soon the solution will arrive and the problem or challenge resolved. Never feel too big to ask or seek for solution from someone.

GUILT FEELING

Guilt feeling is a free passport to weak morale and it leads you to lack of motivation, without motivation man is at failure naturally. Most people whenever life throw them challenges, the sudden feeling of guilt will over shadow them and they assume failure immediately without even giving it any try. Guilt feeling is demonic, don't ever feel guilty at any circumstance and never allow anyone to make you feel guilty. Inciting guilt feeling on someone is the easiest way to manipulate or intimidate that person. Anyone that succeeded in making you feel guilty automatically has taken control over you no matter how smart you think you are.

One way to remain focus in life and fully utilize your God given potential is to do away with guilt feelings and self condemnation. Condemnation of self makes one feel incapacitated to do something or a particular thing. To be resilient or strong through life you have to do away with any form of self guilt or condemnation. It is very destructive and can damage any destiny. When things are not working your way, ask yourself; what must i do? How can i do it? If these questions keep ringing in your mind, believe me the solution will pop-up within your subconscious mind.

Guilt feelings are like regret over that situation or issue that pose itself as challenge to you. Never have any sense of regret whenever you fall short of anything, rather celebrate it. If you believe failure is only a sign or indication that you need to try more, just as it is in its real sense you will overcome any trial. Failure is only a respond that you need to try another way to make it work; so even failure deserve to be celebrated because you now know a way of not doing it right. In life most successful people had failed over and over again. The only different between them and the true failures, is that they never quit at any of those point and that is why they became successful. If successful people feel guilt when they are challenged, they will never end up at success in their endeavours. A guilt feeling takes no one to the zenith of their pursuit or purpose.

We must learn to believe that failure is part of a success story of any greatness. Whenever you try a new thing is either you fail or get it right; but whichever way it turns out to be, always see both results as evidence of applied effort. Everyone that has succeeded on something had failed at some point in their lives. But they never quit when they experience any form of failure on their way to destiny. Success is an accomplishment of a desired goal, task or assignment. But before you accomplish that goal or task there could be failure along the line, the ability to keep moving forward is the resilient you need to achieve your God given potential and fully manifest your purpose in life.

UNFORGIVENESS

A state of un-forgiveness is like carrying a heavy burden, a burden that the victims bring upon themselves when they navigate through this world in greed and supremacy. Because they clench their minds only on what they can get out of life, instead of what they can give to life to discover themselves and purpose of creation, so they term to be unforgiveable. Forgiveness can lighten this burden. The benefits of forgiveness may go beyond the constructive consequences that have been established in the psychological and health domain of the mind and life. Forgivers perceive a less daunting world, and perform better on challenging physical and mental tasks.

One most important tools for resilient in the journey of life is forgiveness. Until you forgive you will remain in bondage of life. To escape the bondage of life or the bondage of the mind you need to learn how to forgive easily. Forgiveness enriches the soul and makes your mind and thought grow positively. The lack of forgiveness leads to stagnation and bitterness. The more bitter you feel about things, the more your ability to think positively declines and it leads to reduction in productivity. It is the easiest way to get drained in your potential or ability. It is a destiny killer; it can delay a destiny for a life time if not checked.

Forgiveness is so important because it helps you gain back your right mind. Whenever something goes wrong around you or someone hurts you, please try and forgive as soon as possible to get back your thought in the right order. May be someone hurts you or you made mistake on something or any form, forgive yourself and forgive the person if it was cause by someone. Forgiveness is strength; once you have it you can overcome any life challenge or obstacle in life.

The first thing the enemy (devil) place in your mind is guilt feelings and lack of forgiveness. Remember the devil is a thief; that came to steal, to kill and to destroy. So never allow him to steal your positive thought away, because it will be exchange with negative once that will destroy you or kill you. Once you lack forgiveness your potential will be put on hold and until you forgive you can't think right in order to get going towards your destiny. It is a real destiny stopper, so get rid of it if you must succeed in life. No matter what went wrong always forgive.

To get in line with destiny you must forgive faster to achieve your God given potential and it makes you resilient to life challenges. When you forgive faster you are helping yourself to remain focus, because anyone that is expose to humanity must at one point or another get upset either by people attitude or actions. But you must keep positive by forgiving. You have all it takes to achieve your dreams or a great destiny if you make forgiveness a part of your life. When forgiveness is part of you, nothing hurts your emotions again. People will think you are emotionless and that the realm you need to operate to fully resist life challenges.

To achieve your purpose or grow your grains of potentials and succeed in life it is necessary you make forgiveness a character. In life you must learn to forgive everyone; the once that didn't channel you to your purpose when you where much younger like your guardians or parents you must forgive them; you must forgive yourself for not being able to discover your purpose early enough; you must forgive your friends that have in one way or another act like a stopper to your true potential through peep influence; you must forgive all your relationship, be it your director in the office you always complain about, your lecturer at school that made you hate a particular course of study, that young man or lady that disappoint your date etcetera. Forgiveness helps you to clean up the mess on your mind, the negative thought and all. It helps you to concentrate, resist and achieve your all desires and aims; it helps you fully utilize your potentials and your dreams will be fast achievable when you make forgiveness a part of you; it helps you adapt to all situations and circumstances; it helps you to resist negative thoughts that can pull you down or make you not to live up to your dreams.

Forgiveness helps you to develop a resilient or strength that will keep you unshakeable in every situation or condition you may find yourself. It is the strength that helps you to develop your unique talent. It's almost mandatory that people will oppose you at one stage or another in life. In such, only forgiveness can keep you going.

In every individual living on the surface of the earth; only two thoughts are dominant, the positive and negative thought. The positive thought helps you to grow in your potential while the negative thought either frustrate you or destroy your destiny. In most cases negative thoughts leads one to destruction. Really there is nothing good that comes out of a negative thought. To resist life challenges you must do away with negative imaginations, lack of forgiveness and self justification. Once you resist them you will be left with only positive thought and that will help you to locate your purpose and destiny faster than you can imagine. Then your grains of potentials will fully grow to maturity and destiny achievable. Forgiveness comforts the soul and makes you explore life effectively.

JEALOUSY

Jealousy is a distraction in disguise. It makes the victim always seek a way to justify their thoughts and actions or accuse others negatively. Before the act of jealousy, the thought is conceived and nurtured as envy. During all this process, the mind that suppose to convey positive thought that can enable productivity and perhaps enable you to discover your potentials will be put on hold. Whenever anyone gets to this cross road their thoughts for positive things are weakened or dominated by negative imaginations, which automatically leads them to failure or lack of purpose in life. The easiest way to shut you out of divine purpose is through jealousy, bitterness and un-forgiveness. None of these are good for you if you must reach destiny or discover your potentials in life. Everybody on earth has a specific assignment to accomplish, so don't let jealousy push you out of your divine calling. While jealousy destroys your ability for positive thinking, it as well make you vulnerable to external constraints; like un-healthy competition, crimes, wicked actions and other social vices. It can cause depression if not put to check; it leads to easy thought of feeling defeated and leads you to drugs and drunkenness.

Jealousy destroys life and resilience, thereby causing you moral discomfort. Because it built up your negative thoughts, that leads you to negative actions. The thought of envy can lead you to lose appetite and ill health. With it you lose courage and enthusiasm to move on in life. It can lead to gossip, negative actions and unnecessary reactions if not checked. It is a destiny killer.

For you to discover your grains of potential or resist life challenges effectively you must check your thought regularly against envy, bitterness, grudges, un-forgiveness etcetera to fully put to use your potentials. Do you know jealousy can lead to youth restiveness if it occurs in a group of individuals? It can hamper their pursuit for credibility and actualization of purpose. It can destroy ones career or profession if the destructive act of jealousy it's being carried out. Some people mentor you to hate others through their words and this can lead you to jealous the person, without your knowing your thought about the person will be negative, you definitely will never see anything good about the person. Let me make this clear to you, everybody on earth have both good and bad aspect in their character. So don't allow anyone to tell you someone it's bad or too good. But i know one thing every human is good until they allow their negative emotions to overpower their positive thought. Once they did; their career, their potential and their sense of humour everything will go down the drain.

It is so vital that you do away with jealousy by every means possible, either through constant mediations (enabling your positive thought to overpower the negative) or get busy always. Jealousy is one attitude that can make you unable to discover yourself or grains of potential. It can push you out of destiny or out of purpose through impatient. It can make you very unproductive, cause you pain and sorrow often times when the actions are being carried out. It makes you unwise and destroys your positive imaginations. It makes you unreceptive to challenges and causes you problems. Jealousy is in no way a good thing, so desist from it and be more adaptive and resilient in life to challenges that threatens your pursuit of destiny. Because jealousy damage inter-human relationships, friendship, progress and cause lack of understanding. To actualise or discover your grains of potentials you have to do away with jealous as a matter of urgency if you really want to be useful in life. Though for most people it cannot be completely destroy but it could still be manage at the level of envy, believe me better you don't make the aim of your envy negative if you must be an achiever. Some justify themselves by saying is human nature to envy, but i tell you envy or jealousy is demonic is never and will not be good for human growth. There is a substitute for envy and that is appreciation, instead you envy try appreciation. You can't have everything, appreciate what you don't and never envy someone that has it. You really do yourself no good by envying someone else.

GRUDGES

This is an ill feeling about someone you had a clash with. When this feeling persist in your mind it can deprive you from putting your potential to effective use or even in most cases you may not discover it. Grudge feelings can destroy your focus and concentration in life to pursuit your divine purpose, in which it can prevent you from discovering your grains of potentials lying within you. It can make you quit half way into any endeavour, project or occupation. It destroys relationships between people. Its feeling is very dangerous to the mind and often leads to negative thoughts that can make life miserable for its victim. Often time's people hurt you no matter how careful or alone you wish to stay, there are always issues that can upset you through interaction and communication with people. So it's better you build your mind with such understanding that if you must be happy living you must make forgiveness a way of life.

Forgiveness is the best substitute for grudge feeling that can aid you laugher and happiness. If your heart fails to merry you're automatically asking for failure in life. One thing is compulsory in life people must mock you, insult you and abuse you when you are down still trying to locate your purpose in life. Only successful people enjoy affluence so don't be down and expect respect or honour from anybody. Quietly and patiently think your way out of your misery; don't ever feel humiliated by what or how people treat you. Mockery is normal for anyone that is still down, absorb it and let that pain propel you to discover yourself. Many people that keep grudges are mostly as a result of feeling humiliated or insulted. Remember one thing your grudge feeling don't change anything, it only worsen the situation, because your mind and soul are subject to feeling of anger and pain. When you are angry you can't think well. Most mistakes people make in life is mostly when they are angry, anger don't change anything, it only suffer the mind and make it wallow continuously on negative thought. To escape from this grudge feeling and be resilient to the challenges of life, i want you to know one thing every problem has an expiring date if you keep on keeping on. Don't rest until you are a success.

Only successful people are allowed to take rest, because everybody at the bottom wants to be on top, remember if you are at the bottom you have countless competitors and obstacles. How then can you take upon yourself such a burden called grudge? If you ever do, do you think you will ever come out successful? Many people call devil this devil that, most often the closest devil is your negative thought. If you are continuously thinking positive soon you will realise that this devil people bound and cast is only a mirage it really don't exist if your heart is pure and clean. There is no strength compared to being positive about life, it give you room to strategise and to monitor situation effectively. Positive mindset destroys fear and you can only be dominated or subdue when you are in fear, then you can be easily manipulated. Grudge feeling can create fear and suspicion in you.

Love is strength and it always win, even where prayer fails, love wins. Let love rain in your heart it will produce seeds that you least expect are inside of you and will enable your positive thinking to replace that grudge feeling with love. It will make you a better person and help you to adapt adequately in the affairs of your life. Resilient is not in the absent of challenges, it's only the ability to withstand those challenges that destroys productivity and growth. Without resisting them you could end up in stagnation in life. To put your grains of potentials to effective use you must ensure you do away with negative thought like grudge by every means possible. Some years ago i decide that nothing will ever upset me or make me angry to lose focus, and do you know that it works? I was able to stay away from gossip and bitterness. A lot of things in life will upset you if you fail to make this decision, "that nobody on flesh and blood can ever provoke you or get you mad to lose focus of where you want to be".

This decision will automatically make you stay away from being angry for a long time that can cause you bitterness, pain or thought of evil. Another thing is don't be judgemental and always assume people make mistakes including you. Once you are able to see things from this other angle, you feel less worried about what people deed to upset you, who is trying to humiliate you or accuse you. These are simple attitude to resist temptation and challenges. They help you to adapt very well in life and relationship. They always help you to discover who you truly are and what you can offer. Can you imagine a society where everybody behaves the same way? Nothing will ever work in such society; do you know why? Our difference is why we need each other. Without those features that makes us different; why will there be anything like transactions, team work and union? If you have everything you need, there will be no need for friends or even relatives, that why nobody has it all.

So we human can inter relate among ourselves and achieve greater things together. Nobody exists effectively in isolation; companionship is a great strength and can keep you warm and happy. So why keep malice and grudge for the privilege you where only given to inter relate with others. Why often found fault in people. Just believe no one is perfect and let go of any anger or pain that anyone might have caused you. It will help you withstand challenges and will make you happier and more productive. With joy you can locate destiny as easy as possible, you get more out of life when you are happy and in pure state of mind.

To remain ever happy in life, don't ever think that life is fair. This understanding gives you the awareness to keep boundaries and continuously be on guard. Guarding your thoughts and actions enable you to escape freely from those negative things that may lead you to wrong directions or trouble. Your life is what you feed your mind. How do i mean? If you feed your mind with negative thoughts your life will go down the drain. In the other hand if you feed your mind with positive thoughts your life will flourish and produce good fruits. You must be willing to think positively and do positive things. Our thoughts define our actions. You can't be thinking negatively and be acting positively. You can't have grudge feeling about someone and expect to love that person or act nicely to the person. A lot of things you can't pretend about in life. So i request you to keep a clean heart and mind to enable more positive thoughts if you must resist life challenges and discover your grains of potential and put them into effective use.

Sometimes expecting too much from people can lead you to grudge feelings, so don't expect too much from anybody even your parents. If they offer you help let it be a plus. Create this mind set, "Nobody is responsible for your life but you", it gives you the sense to always be grateful and appreciative to people and most time make room for more support and assistant. When you take responsibility of your life it give you the sense of self believe and without you believing in yourself you can't resist any challenge in life. When you always need people to assist you that when you begin to receive disappointment, promise and fail; which will lead you to feeling bad or having grudges for them.

Anything you want out of life, make sure you are prepared to undertake it. That gives you alternate plans in case you being neglected or disappointed, which will build up your resilience force to overcome any challenge along the way. Remember trees don't beg for rain, it fall on them when the cloud lose it weight or when the gardener decides. Just as men, we are like trees, whatever help you get from others is because God shows his mercy or grace on you. This understanding will make you firm and strong about the things of life and also enables you to escape grudge feelings.

Believe in yourself even when nobody believes in you; focus on where you are going when you get there people will definitely love you not only for your success but for believing in you. To be resilient in life and adapt fully to life situations, you must do away with grudge feelings or any form of negative thought. Remember two days are most important in a man's life, the day he was born and the day he discovers the purpose for his creation. You can only be mastery in your calling and you discover yourself when your heart and mind is pure. Blessed are the pure in heart for they shall see God. Your destiny can only be communicated to you by God. When your heart or mind is not pure or positive, you can never locate your purpose. Remember seeds dies even before germinating, your destiny can only die when negative thought over flood your mind, and grudge feeling is one of such negative feeling that can hamper your discovery of purpose. Often times weaken your ability to withstand challenges.

Chapter 4

DECISION AND DISCIPLINE

Seeds must be on good soil to grow and produce well;
growth is not in the absent of discipline and right decision

Decision is the very first step to take when trying to achieve a purpose, but it takes discipline to keep on track. Discipline works with your attitude and they are very relative. They are the parts of the elements that boost your ability to attain any height in life. Whatever decision you make in life back it up with discipline. It's not enough to be motivated, motivation encourages decisions. Motivation can only get you going, but discipline keeps you growing. Everyone likes to be victorious, so victory is a good companion but you need understanding and discipline to keep it longer than enough.

Growth is intentional not accidental, so when making decision on that career, job or profession back it up with discipline. For anyone to achieve destiny he must decide what he wants. One major characteristic of the great is the ability to make decision and take responsibilities for their actions. Be in charge of yourself, believe in yourself and make decision on how to do your things. Don't be afraid to make decision because of the fear of failure. Failure is only a feedback that you can try it in another way. Make failure your friend; it gives you courage to try more things. And remember good friends don't hurt and friendship breaks when one party steps aside. You automatically steps aside of failure when you succeeds. But never be afraid of failure, friends don't fear each other else they can't be called friends.

The world today needs men and women who are highly focused, determine and goal driven with the ability to make decisions and take responsibility for their actions. So don't be left out, start making decision with the right discipline as follow up. When you say "yes" let it be "yes". No matter what life challenged you with? Challenges are temporary, and no challenge will ever come to you that you don't have the ability to overcome. All a seed needs to grow to become a plant is within the seed. The wind doesn't stop it from getting to maturity if its root is firm enough to withstand the forces of the wind. Do you know the height of a plant is measure by the strength of his root and stem? Have you ever asked yourself why desert plants don't grow too tall? It's because their roots don't go too deep into the soil. So don't be afraid of any challenge you may encounter out of your decision. They are all part of your life circle. So make decision today and ensure that you don't go out of course, make sure you tread carefully by disciplining yourself. Just as plants are not expected to grow more than the strength of their roots and stem. As someone with focus be ready to proof to the world that your decisions are right by accompany them with the right or required discipline it needed to see the light of the day. To achieve something new, you must do something new. To achieve a new height you must decide to do something you never done before. Dreaming is not satisfying if you're not living it. To live in your dream you must become the person of your dreams.

I remember during my industrial training, when i was given a software program codes to memorise for two weeks and teach others. So i had to discipline myself by reading eighteen hours (18hours) everyday in order to master the syntax. It takes extra effort to achieve or attain extra ordinary height don't let anyone deceive you. Some people may tell you life is easy, listen to me they lied. Life is tough, but the good thing about it is; tough times don't last, that challenge has expiring date.

There is no cheap victory, without the required amount of effort that will stand the taste of time. If you want to shine like the sun be prepared to burn like one. You need challenges in life for God to glory himself in you, don't run from it. They are necessary for you to truly enjoy your success or victory.

When i was imparting the knowledge i got from reading the programs, everybody was saying you are just very good at it. Everyone appreciated it, even the students in the cooperate class (Bank Executives) i was taking. They never knew i was still a student that is just doing his Industrial Attachment, most of them where asking for personal coaching. That is what confronting challenges and taking decision can make out of you. You are more than how you see yourself, welcome that challenge and give it extra time

68

and thinking you must succeed. Challenges don't kill they can only make you better, stop being afraid of the unknown. When you get to the bridge you will definitely get a way to cross it just take that decision and remain focus.

Don't be scared of what comes next; only prepare your mind to face it squarely. The different between a failure and victory; is that failures seek a cheap way, but when they can't fine it they quit. But victorious people discipline themselves to withstand whatever may come next and proffer solution to tackle any challenge that may arise. Preparing the mind is one secret of victorious people, not that they never had challenges. It takes discipline to be adequately prepared. All birds seek shelter during the rain but the eagle flies above the cloud to avoid the rain. You need extra effort to be distinguished, just as the eagle. Greatness lays on the un-usual not the casual. Be more dedicated to make solid achievement than running after synthetic happiness.

In other to actualise your God given potentials in relationship to your calling or endeavour you need to make reasonable decisions, but before these decisions can yield fruits you require some level of discipline to enforce it. Every decision demands discipline to follow up effectively. Discipline is like a law that must be met if decision will be effective. Just like seeds, they require good soil to grow and to become plant. Even fish require water to live.

Natural laws can't be violated. If you want a seed to produce good harvest you need to prepare the soil very well for its growth. Same goes to making effective decision; you require discipline to enforce it. If you want to fail you don't need discipline or any form of effort. If you are at the ground you need nothing to remain on the ground, but if you must leave the ground you will require effort to pull you up. Do you know why i am over stressing the need of discipline in decision making? Challenges are constant contender with destiny and our decisions as human. Discipline is very essential tool to compliment decision, most decisions in life requires follow up. When you make decisions take actions and stay put on that particular decision to see it's manifested. Now you know that challenges are in constant contention with your purpose, you need to make wise decision and give your all to see it through. With discipline you can decide or regulate what happens around you.

Just as a farmer often decides to get rid of the weed on his farm land to enable his crops grow well and produce good fruit, so you need to discipline yourself in a lot of things to ensure your decisions see the light of the day. It's not enough to have a dream, because if your dreams never come through who will ever know you had a dream? No matter what you cooking, if the food it's not served your guest will remain hungry. A food can only be good cook if it's well cooked, a half cooked can never be a good cook. You don't use words to console a hungry man, the world is hungry to see what you got on your inside, they want to know if your decisions are right, so discipline yourself to proof you have got something to offer. Man's decisions determines how far or fortunate they become, some of our decision could be right, but without discipline to see it through they may end up as trash or wasted effort. We will consider some very few important decision every man should make to better their lives and direct their focus, like i have being saying these decisions need discipline also to see it through. And there are as follows;

MAKE OUT TIME WITH GOD IN FELLOWSHIP

Anything you need you don't have option for it. On like the things you want. Man needs God, just as fish needs water and seed needs the soil to grow and produce better fruits. God is never an option is a must do. Do you know you grow in wisdom just by fellowshipping with God? Even only by reading your bible daily, you can experience a whole lot of mind transformation. The fear of God makes you wise, without wisdom where do you think you are going with that purpose? It's like a plane without a pilot, if you as the passenger decides to pilot the plane be ready to crash soon. Without God as your guide you will crash no matter how gifted you are.

Challenges are darkness of life they have senses and they know when God is by your side, they naturally fuses out. Challenges become allergic to you when you are in God and God in you. God is a great strength if you have him, you have this boldness to confront anything and the will power to do mighty things. There are sometime your actions surprises you and you may be asking yourself how did i really achieved this, that how God works within us. Listen to me if you don't know how to keep long time with God or you yet to make out time for God, Start with this simple tips; when you are stepping out of your house pray to God to guide you, when you want to eat pray God satisfy you with the meal. When you succeed in anything thank God first, when you are in trouble ask God what to do first. Before you sleep, travel or engage in anything as God to take absolute charge. Learn to give away yourself to God.

If you continue to seek God again and again soon it will become a habit and your life will begin to take a new shape. Don't ever be in any form of haste to forget to acknowledge God. Seed don't grow in tiles; they must be in the soil to germinate. They are forces contending with your destiny and your decision is your bailout. Decide and give your life and everything about you to God, because is the safest place it can be. If you think there is no power anywhere, i want you to try this; even it's for only a month.

Every morning and night before the day break completely and before the night falls. Be in a position where you can see the sky. Watch it with curiosity and try to imagine how it looks, get the picture for each day, do it for one month. You will realise that there is never a morning or night that had the same formation or have the same similarity. Every day is God's day but the day you connect to him is your day. A lot of forces contend with the glory God have prepared for us, but when we connect to God absolutely those forces disappears. The beauty of the sky alone is enough for you to begin to acknowledge God in your life. If the changes you see on the sky every day begin to happen in your life how glorious will your life be? Friend's there is God and it's supreme over all. He is in charge of the universe. Every maker of a thing is proud of what he made. God is very proud of you, only you running away from him. Connect to him and you will experience a whole lot of transformation you never imagine possible. Make out time for him; he is already waiting for you to decide and to take that step.

The universe is ready to bring you that desires of your heart, but you could be blinded about the true knowledge of God, he commands and the universe obeys. God has everything you need and the good news is he is ready to give to you, because he loves you. All he wants from you is to love him back and follow his leading. Please get close to him, no one ever regret of knowing or serving God. Fish don't regret of being in the water, they naturally love water. You need to naturally accept the fact that "you can't do without God". Without God you are nothing. If you truly believe this words, don't only say it, act on it. Anything you knew you can't do without, naturally you seek it and when you found it, you do everything to keep it. Do same in your relationship with God you will be amazed how fast things will change around you. Do you know without God "nothing that was made that is truly made"? Mediate on this word; "without God nothing that was made that is truly made". Meaning, anytime anything that God made lose sight with God it loses its value. It can't stand the taste of time alone; it must have the hand of God at work in it; including our dreams and destiny. They can only be truly made visible by the hand of God.

Acknowledging God in once life is wisdom. Some say, why do believers still have challenges? Like I told you challenges are normal to life. Everyone must have challenge, but there is assurance from God; that no challenge will ever come to you that you don't have the capacity to overcome. So that alone put you ahead, you already have the awareness that you are bigger than that problem you facing right now. Make the right decision and discipline yourself by acknowledging God in that situation first. Anytime you face a tough situation, first acknowledge God with it. God sees everything, so he knows the situation you are in right now. But he wants to see how humble you could be to acknowledge him first. He is waiting for you to bring it onto him. He said come to me all you with heavy burden and i will give you rest.

There is rest with God always. Let God take over that challenge you begin to experience a smooth ride through life and that your purpose. Make this decision to always make God your first choice of solution and your guide. God is light, if you welcome him into your affairs he will light up your life. When you become light, naturally that darkness that have being chasing you in form of challenges will fuses away. Because light don't contest with darkness. At the arrival of light darkness disappears.

Do you know working with God destroys negative thoughts; in fact mediating on God's word is the easiest way to get rid of negative thought. It gives wisdom and insight for divine direction. It shows you where to go and how to go about it. Guess everybody needs to know where to go with their lives and how to go about it. God is all you need to be informed and to conquer. Its wisdom to make the decision to always acknowledge God in your life, you require discipline to stay turn every time in continuous acknowledgement of God in your life and affairs. Believe me at the end of it all you definitely will be happy you did.

RIGHT CHOICE OF ASSOCIATION

Choose your friends wisely, no man can exist alone but the right choice of friends matters a lot. They are friends that destroy every potential in you (as a result of peep influence). Who we associate with, what we associate with determines how far we can go in life. Friends are support, they are suppose to build and make you better, if in your present relationship you not getting this feedback then you are on the wrong association. You need people to achieve your purpose, but yet only people that understand your purpose and are willing to act as support to you is truly needed.

It is foolishness to have a truck load on a taxi. Don't make friends with luggages, when you already have your heavy load on you. Rather make friends with drivers that can at least carry some of your luggage or when they can't, they will at least direct or channel you on the right part to go. If you are the wisest person among your friends you don't yet have a friend, the day challenges will set in you will realise the truth behind this words. If every company you keep add value to you, soon you will grow so tall. There is a saying; Show me your friends and i will tell you who you are, Birds of same feather flop together. Don't be an eagle and fly with vulture or pigeon, look for eagles to fly with.

If a seed is found among weeds it can't grow well. Bad friends are like weeds to your grains of potential, either they kill your potential during growth or they burry it without it seeing the light of the day. So many great minds are in the grave because of wrong association; their destiny was just cut short. Deciding who to bring into your boat is one of the most courageous and beneficial decision anyone can make, once you get the right people your boat will never sink. When challenges overpower you is because your strength is little, not that the challenge was too much. Friends are strength and support in times of need. They play a vital role in building up your destiny, same you are to them, that is why you are called friends.

So, when your friends are like weeds to your grains of potential, they drain you up without your knowing. You don't expect seed to germinate where there are too many weeds contending with it, even if it germinates, it can't survival the advent condition to grow to become a great plant.

Once you notice your friends are becoming weed to your potentials give way. Don't say they will change, weeds don't become crops. They grow and become stronger weeds; crops don't grow together with weeds and expect to produce good fruit. That is why the farmer always weeds their farm land to enable the crop to grow well. It is wisdom to stay away from friends that are like weeds to our grains of potentials. You have an enviable destiny, your job is to protect it and nurture it to maturity.

At different levels you are expected to keep different kinds of relationship. Babes' best friends are their mother or parents, when they get into school their play group. Often this play group is monitored by their teachers or guardians, and they are often thought and been corrected by them. As this child grows he begins to make use of his senses and less advice or guide could be needed. He is not always with his guardian or under the constant watch of his teachers. This is where he begins to be influence by friends or close associates.

Teenage level is very important, in fact is the most crucial level. You know why? The child will begin to compare what the guardians have implanted in him, and what he sees from among friends and the society. If he is more comfortable with what his teenage friends or the society is saying, definitely he will accept their ways. That could lead him out of purpose and destroy him like weeds to the crop. Whenever you tell a child something give him or her reasons and be very sincere with your reason. Kids of these days are very smart and they are exposed to a lot of things. Most of which are driven by the societal believes and norm. There is a saying; "teach a child the way he should grow so that when he grows he will not depart from it".

Relationships build or break people; it can ruin your life, career or business with its negative influence. It can also aid you to discover your true potentials, so it's very important you make the right decision when choosing friends or associate. Some friends can make you see beyond where you are now; they can even make you more resilient to challenges if you learn their strategies. They can make you to dream more and see success in any situation. They can inspire you to grow; they can challenge you to always do better.

Keeping friends is not a bad thing only bad friends are truly dangerous. They prevent you from achieving your goals and could stop you half way if not checked. Most of them are truly not friends but they wear the image of friends only to monitor you and when you need their counsel they drive you out of purpose immediately. Some friends see it as a privilege to mislead you, and they rejoice at doing it behind your back. So when you seek advice from someone digest it first (think over it) don't just begin to act on it. Some could be just for their selfish interest. Most people you call friends are benefactors and competitors, they contend with you at every level. A competitor can't guide you well, because they don't want you to be better than them. Make friends with people that have respect for friendship and they see you as a friend, not those that see you as a traitor or competitor. Only then you can be of great help to one another and your grains of potentials will be discovered and put to effective use. Decision on the choice of friends or association is very important to self actualisation.

ALWAYS BE IN CHARGE OF YOURSELF

When the outcome of your decision is not favourable, nobody will ever agree that they gave you the advice that leads you to it. Even when they agreed, they will never bear the consequences with you. So, no matter the situation be in charge of your actions. People could advice you, but believe me the outcome of your actions are basically and truly yours. When its positive people will claim to have advised you rightly, it takes a sincere friend to share the blames but not the pain. You bear the consequence of your actions, even when they are being motivated by others. This doesn't mean you will not be taking actions, but be responsible for your actions; be in charge of thought and actions. Burden is like a naked wire, just as nobody in his right senses goes to a naked wire to safe the other. So it is to a burden, nobody share in your burden or pain just to aid you help. The best they can do is to console you or pity you.

You are the driver of your destiny, why God directs your part and light up your ways so you can see clearly. So, it's up to you to take charge of your destiny by being absolute responsible of the outcome of your life. You are the sole architect to your life, what you make out of it is what you get from it. That why you need to be in charge, guard your thought, because from it are issues of life that can either make you better or break you to pieces.

The master plan or blue print of your destiny lies within your thought, what you accomplish at the end is always as a result of what you had nurtured in your mind as thought. Be positive always, only positive minded people achieve destiny. Don't ever give anybody control over your destiny, it's the easiest way to subject you to control and enslavement. Make your choices and decision, so that when ever things went wrong you know it was truly your decision. Never allow anyone to push you over or push you into what you are not truly motivated to accomplish. Without your motivation in it you can't gain mastery, it will only be time wastage. If you must discover your grains of potentials lying within you, you must fully be responsible of your life and actions.

MAKE OUT TIME TO THINK OR MEDITIATE

Being in charge of you is not in absent of good thinking. If you don't think well, your decisions will always be wrong no matter how placed you are in the society. A good decision is a product of good thinking. Think over your plans before you execute them, think over your words before you use them. Words are like sword; it can make or break relationships. Good thinking is very important to everyone that wants to achieve any purpose.

Remember you are a product of your thought. Smart people pay others to think for them, but they will still think over the choices available. There is really no easy way out of not making effective use of your thought. You need to meditate on your plans often before its being executed. Right thinking gives you a better understanding and broadens your vision.

Thinking provides the right strategic frame work that will energize you for great accomplishment. Great thoughts are builder of great destiny. Thinking gives birth to ideas and imaginations that channel your focus to achieve your purpose and as well discover your purpose in life. Creativity begins with good thought. Thinking and meditation gives room for good planning and execution, because everything you need to get to your destination or destiny as a person is already deposited in you. A seed has the capacity to become a tree, all that its needed for the seed to become a tree is already in the seed. But the seed needs water, soil nutrients and sunlight to germinate, just as the seed you need good thought (positive thought) among other things to get to your destiny and make a great future. Only good thinking can open a man to endless possibilities.

Meditations surpasses negative thought, that why is good to meditate, it will always enrich the mind with positive thoughts. It's this feeling of deeper thought that gives you true understanding of your existence. Make meditation an essential part of your daily life, because it calms the mind. This is done in the silence of the soul, mind and body. Those that live well think right. To make fortune and success your state of mind must be dominated with positive thought. Make out time to think, this one decision you be happy that you made. After everyday work or function, get yourself on a quiet corner and meditate or think over what you have really done. If you fall short of anything you should have done right, that is the time to verify those mistake and re-strategize.

One good thing about thinking or meditation, is that it gives you room for correction and reconciliation with divinity and men. Continuous meditation eliminates every form of negative thought in your mind and enables you to growth both physically and spiritually. If you make this a habit you will be in constant connection with yourself, you begin to discover who you truly are.

MAKE DECISION TO ALWAYS READ

When you stop reading you stop growing, Information is light. Most profitable and most accessible means to acquire the knowledge of a thing or anything is reading. Reading broadens you in all areas of life. It builds you up, it energizes you, it guides you and it gives you understanding and knowledge. Reading is the most accessible medium for growth in childhood. It habit is such rewarding. It enables you to explore the universe from a spot with imagination and understanding. The understanding you derive from reading can aid you to discover yourself, even discover other new things.

Reading broaden your understanding, so it's very good to cultivate the habit of reading; anybody that can read at all, can read a whole lots every day; like journals, resource materials, sign post, From media houses and Street. It's very necessary we make a decision to engage in this practice with all enthusiasm like as if our growth depends on it, because it truly does. The growth reading offers the mind, our actions and our thinking is so transformational, it brings about personal change in a whole lot of ways. When you make reading a habit you will never run short of ideas. Ideas are indicators that can lead anyone to destiny, and it's often gotten through reading. Ideas also inspire men to dream.

Growth is advancement gotten from change. The mind also grows, because it changes, and this change is from learning new things. The mind and the brain works together to connect effectively with materials you read. The more you read the more understanding you gain. The more you read the better you speak and the more informed you become. Anyone that must discover his potentials and work in divine purpose must read materials and also make reading a habit. Reading becomes enjoyable if you make it a habit. Make a decision to always read something that will grow you one step forward in life and in your profession or career. With daily reading you can grow in your profession faster and you can discover your hidden potentials, you can as well get wisdom into new things and a whole lot of things.

MAKE FINANCIAL DECISON

With good check and balances in your financial planning you are more willing and confident to chase your purpose in life. Money is like a fuel to destiny. As water is important to a plant in the field so its money to a man's life, without money any destiny is helpless, every destiny requires financial support to get going. With good financial decision you be ever ready to take any step that can move you to next level. Money gives confident and every man need confident to achieve destiny.

You may not have all the money in the world before you can start chasing destiny, but you need to have financial support just as the plant need water. Water or rain makes the plant flourish, so money makes destiny flourish. Good financial decision is not limited to how you spend your money; it also on the kind of investment you make how you build your financial ladder, your saving and the things you spend your money on. With good financial discipline you can avoid wasteful spending.

Most people purchase things they never need. Some buy things to show off not that they truly need them. You learn to spend money on things you really need and not for the sake of pleasing people. Get what you are comfortable with. Most of the things we acquire are mainly for the attraction we get from them not because we truly need them, but if you can discipline yourself and make decision to get only what you need. Before time you be saving a whole lot of money for building up your purpose.

For you to remain balance and unshaken in life you need to always have financial security. This step will always create ways for financial inflow in your life and investment. It is very necessary no matter your income to limit spending of any kind. A good financial planning can boost your confident in life to chase your destiny with all momentum required. Always having money to fall back on is always a strength that is why is very important to save. It help your investment and growing of your wealth. Money grows but it can only grow through savings and investment. No matter what you earn if you have no good financial plans it will always not be enough. Money is never enough without a good financial decision. To discover your destiny you require some level of financial decisions and discipline, contentment comes mostly through financial availability to chase your purpose. Some men can't be restful without any money in their bag. Going broke so often can cause delay of purpose. Because even to engage in some training that will grow you one step forward you require money. To even further your studies you need money and even feed yourself requires money as well. So it's very necessary you plan your finance by making good financial decisions to gain momentum and confident to chase your dreams and achieve your desired goals.

Irregular inflow and outflow of money can wreck a life or even an organisation. It can also lead to scarcity of resources that can aid you to discover your grains of potential. For you to get really well in life there must be good financial planning to keep at constant pace with your purpose. Money is a motivation for any man, it sustain life and makes it better. So the better your financial plans the better your life and the more you're confident to discover your purpose in life.

DECISION ON THINGS WE EAT

Food builds the body and supplies it with the required nutrient. What we feed our body system determines our health. Our health determines how far we can go in life. The dead don't have destiny, and they can't chase any dream. Sickness limits the strength of a man and as well weakens the cells of the body. If one is sick, his immune system is weak and lead to malfunctioning of some organs in the body.

A sick man is not purpose driven even when he has plans, the capacity and ability required will not be available for him to enforce his plans. Most often the things we feed our body system weakens or strengthens it. It's very good to be selective; some food could be poison to Mr A and a Nutrient to Mr B. Is good to fine out those food that makes you function well and make them part of your diet. Everything call food can't be good for everyone. So, definitely there are foods that are good for you. Some food cause you sleep and weakness, some gives you strength or strengthens you. So it's up to you to make decision on things you feed your body, some food shorten your life span with time and are not good for excessive consumption.

Certainly what we eat adds value to our health and sustains our lives, some cause pain and abnormality when misused. To really accomplish destiny and enjoy life one must be in good health. Most of the things we eat are poison to our health if only we know their effects, some tends to cut life short through infectious diseases and some shift us away from focus. Imagine a student that abuse drugs or it's a drunkard. No matter how good he or she may be, he can't be same compare to when he stays away from them. Life requires regulations, of what we do and even what we eat. That why God has given us wisdom to chose. Chose rightly and make the best out of life. Life is so precious, and man has unlimited possibilities. So, check the things that enter into it, so you don't waste out where there is abundance. To discover our purpose and explore them adequately we must make decisions on the things we feed our body, soul and spirit with.

DISCIPLINE

Discipline is the Attitude that produce consistent growth. It's also a way of subjecting to a system or routine. This is play by the rules attitude. Discipline determines destiny. It makes things sustainable. It enables continuous running of a process through a define pattern. It put you on track for effective application of plans and makes you result oriented. To actualise a plan or keep on a process you must be discipline to grow and to keep growth constant. Whatever decision you made as we earlier discussed you must be very discipline in application. Consistency require discipline to be effective, when making decisions, it takes discipline in the process and procedure to establish victory.

Plants don't need water in hurt sun, so Horticulturist doesn't water them in high humility or heat. They expected to water them at morning and evening. They have cultivated that discipline to enable the plants grow well. So everyone needs discipline to keep decision on check and maximize productivity. If you desire growth in any endeavour be discipline in enforcing your decisions, because discipline makes growth consistent. Discipline put attitude and character on check.

They are some actions when you make decision on them; either to drop them or to acquire them. They necessarily need discipline to be practically enforced. They become policy or part of a process after they are well monitored and thought over a period. These thoughts becomes part of us when we make them part of our decision. The decisions become a way of life through discipline and careful application, which makes growth consistent.

Discipline is needed in every areas of life, it regulate actions and increase growth and performance. There are some common areas in our daily life that requires discipline; like sleeping habit, food habit, our sexuality, our dependency on others and others on us, our attitude towards work etcetera.

There are some signs that are associated with people that lack discipline;

a. They always late at appointment.
b. They waste more time and energy on unproductive ventures.
c. They often follow temporary satisfaction and carnal desires.
d. They make a lot of financial Mistakes.
e. They Defend wrong doing
f. They often have poor performance at work or studies.
g. The society or people don't take them serious.
h. They mismanage resources (No check and balance).

Discipline is very good, but often time it's difficult to be absolutely discipline without understanding these three elements that affects man; the devil, our environment and our flesh. It is wise to build your strength and resistance against these three known enemies if you must succeed or put your potential into effective use. As your thought affect your life, so your environment either makes you become better or worst. Be motivated enough to make your decision and be discipline to keep it consistent no matter the challenges. It is important that anything you decide on be diligent and discipline at it to always remain floating. Discipline is having self control or being in charge of you to follow a procedure or obey law. Diligent and self control guarantees your effective execution of decision. Practicing self-control is a sure way to check growth and make it continuous. It enables us to discover who we truly are. To achieve destiny you must know who you are, pursuit your purpose and achieve it. Discipline help to withstand challenges when they arise. It keep you focus on your aim and devoid distractions.

A way to maintain discipline is to set goals for yourself and pursuit it with all diligence. Believe in your ability and be contented it helps your focus to be strong in chasing your dreams. Everything that have life has its challenges, it either make you or break you. For challenge to make you better you must be discipline and make good decisions.

As is important for a new born baby to cry, so it's important you acknowledge the fact that challenges is part of life. To avoid distractions when challenges come, you must make discipline and diligent part of you. Be ready to obey laws and follow orderliness. Discipline and diligence to a man is like soil and the roots to the plant. For the plant to stand firm its roots must be well fix to the soil to withstand any wind or any environmental hazard. Build your life tree on discipline; your purpose will be fast achievable. Life is challenging but with discipline and diligent the challenges are least visible. Build your life solid foundation on discipline and diligence you become mastery. To achieve your purpose or discover your grains of potentials lying within you discipline is not an option. It's a tool that must be put into effective use to achieve destiny. Discipline helps you to build a character that your destiny requires to blossom.

CHAPTER 5

MATURITY OF GRAINS

Every seeds that can withstand all odds gets to maturity;
Victory lies in the mind of the meek

Maturity is a stage in a process where the object or subject is in its grown stage. Seed grows to maturity, just as animals; this enables them for reproduction in animal or production of flowers in plants. Maturity is applicable for human development process also; like training and learning of new ideas. Maturity makes you better, stronger and structured to undertake responsibility and implement skills. A student that is undergoing the process of Education matures to function after his graduation. Maturity as relate to student implies a satisfactory level of learning when the student is awarded Certificate of learning. To be matured means to be ready to deploy that which is inside of you to achieve a set goal.

Maturity provides the privilege to effectively put to use your acquired skills. When one is matured in a process, procedure or learning; he becomes a useful vessel needed to make a process function freely and effectively.

When seeds mature they begin to produce fruits for harvest. Maturity leads to reproduction, Ones you matured you set to reproduce. You attain the height to give back into the process. Your potentials are becoming visible and appreciable. You become effective on the process, actions required in achieving an aim or a goal has being acquired. Your potentials freely run the process with better skills and developed talents for better results. There are significant of maturity in every endeavour or process, they could be seen as traces or evidence of maturity; these traces are;

CONSISTENCY OF PROCESS

Continuity in a process over some period of time is a great sign of maturity in the process. It enables learning on the process, effective application of decisions and procedure control. Consistent process keeps activities on going, within a planned frame work. Like in seed, if a seed receive water adequately with the right climate the seed must have a great yield during harvest. Before any seed can get to its maturity stage it must have adapt fully to the climate and environmental conditions. Nothing can stand on the way of a seed that have the adequate nutrient and good environment to grow. Same is applicable to human; a diligent man with Willpower can never be stopped. Nothing like a man that makes good decision, discipline and diligent, he will surely discover himself and achieve his goals. I call it the '3Dmotion's rules'. These qualities make every barrier flew. The thought you nurture in your heart is what you become. In a chain process; learning on the process requires your consistency for better performance and effective risk management.

Like seed when they are growing; they resist the wind and heavy out pour of rain time after time, before they get to the maturity stage. They have always kept growing even in the mist of such wind and heavy rain. They keep growing taller; that is process consistency we are talking about. It's the surest way to maturity.

Keep moving on a pace of continuous growth. That will take you to your maturity. In your profession for instant, if you keep on track climbing the ladder soon you will get to the top. But that does not mean there will be no challenges, when you get to the top you may choose to reflect on those challenges if you care, but what this book is saying to you its remain focus, careless about the challenges, think more about ways to the top, what must be done to get there, what possible procedure or process is required. One thing for sure there is always a way out. There is always a way to everything.

Consistency keeps you on track, with continuous innovation and continuous implementation of ideas on the process to achieve excellent result. You become matured when you have monitor and practice the process over some time. Plants don't get matured once by resisting the wind or absorbing high humidity or withstand heavy rain. But by continuous resistance it grows to its matured stage.

Everything new to a man demands him to learn about it. To get new skills you be willing to learn it. To get mastered to the skill you have to be consistent all through the process for effective impartation. Every works of life, every career and every endeavour that is new to our knowledge require us some period of learning. To be mastery we have to be consistent all through the process. This consistency helps also to nurture our potential and discover our gifts and talent why on the process. Every grains of potential you discover, needs to be cultivated before it can grow to maturity. You need to be consistent when on the process to aid you maturity or to achieve your desired result.

CONSISTENCY OF PURPOSE

They are some seeds when they begin to grow they grow straight, but after some time. They will bend, like tomatoes tree or most legume crops. When they bend they fall out of purpose, because they didn't remain consistent to the growth direction. This can lead to reduction of yield, none resilience or low production. This happens to most individual, why chasing their destiny. When the journey gets tough all they do is back out or fall off. It's good to remain consistent in every process of growth with discipline your maturity is achievable.

Though the plants that bend can still be support and still get the require yield at harvest. Like most often the tomatoes tree needs support to stand and produce better yield; so it applied to most situations of man when on course. Ask and it shall be given, seek and you shall found.

If you need help to keep on to the process of self discover or maturity, go all out and ask. Everyone at a point needs support to get on well in life. But never lose focus to bend down or take a bow because of that challenge. Stand up, if you can look up, you can stand up.

Purpose is the willpower that drives any destiny, both organisational and individual. Though in life or a process there could be challenges, but with consistency of purpose you will surely overcome. With consistency of purpose one is conscious of the ways to tackle challenges rather than quitting. Purpose is a very great force within; it's the willpower that keeps saying "yes i can"! "Yes I will overcome"!! That invokes your thought and reasoning towards refined strategies to overcome. Consistency builds strength and groom confident, to confront challenges and still keep to process. The more the challenges invade the better your strategies to overcome, because you have well defined purpose and will do everything to make it work. Elements of the system are expected to put up the best system conflict resolution strategies to keep purpose on course. Through this challenge you will gain knowledge and ideas once you keep your purpose strong.

There is lesson in every challenge if you have a strong purpose to oppose. Without opposition challenges will remain. You need to fight to win and you need to win to be successful. Anytime do make sure, you are prepared to stand up no matter what. Be consistent in that which you are gifted or in that your purpose you will surely get to maturity and become successful. Consistency of purpose makes you unshakable by challenges, because your mind is fix on that which you want to achieve. When you are purpose driven you overcome all odds with persistent and consistent. Nothing stop a man with a define purpose and a clear direction from achieving his aim if he remains consistent.

Don't be scared of failure, every man has failed in one thing or another. Failure is a feedback to try again. Just persist and remain consistent, when you fail, laugh over it, and move on to try again. If you fall, dust your body, get up and start running again. When you have a purpose you have got a 'will' and with your 'will' there is 'power' in you, to make it "willpower".

Before every child can walk, the child must have fall over and over again. Every one that wants to walk in new purpose will experience same to stand firm and walk very tall. So, don't give up because you fail, only ensure you are growing in your knowledge to avoid failure in same kind of challenge next time. The process of consistency gives room to learn on mistakes. To be mature in a process you need to monitor the function and structure of the process. Its step by step learning approach, you take things as they come why you keep on to the purpose. It's a great way to gain mastery in the process, which is maturity you derive through learning on the process. Consistency of purpose enables one to effectively explore those grains of potentials he discovers through the process to maturity.

EFFECTIVE APPLICATION OF PLANS

Every gardener knows that a seed can become tree. They also aware that the seed need to be in the soil, nurtured with nutrient before it can actually become tree. With this in mind they make best possible plans to ensure a great harvest. This is applicable to man's talent and potentials. You have to fellow a routine to nurture your potential when you discover it, which makes it mature and ready to manifest. Those decisions you made and disciplinary measures you took when you discover your grains of potentials are to be effectively applied in the process to guarantee success. Plans that have being tested over time in the process, are re-applied after undergoing much study and believed you to have adequate knowledge to ensure expected result. Once your application of plans is effective your productivity will be efficient for maximum result. Maturity is when you attain the stage when results are maximum's with indication of continuing growth.

Every process is subject to error at initial stage during the learning stage. At this stage plans have not begin to be effectual, then to ensure improvement or growth, plans must be re-organise with better strategy after some period of learning on the process; to become more effective, more proactive and more result oriented. Adequate information's and system resource materials needed to be sorted out for better planning and improvement on the process. When it gets to a stage of maturity, here the plans have being well understood and worked upon, so it has become effective. For example; a university student at his first year, he may have a reading time table, which he decided to use as his daily reading time plans. After his first semester examination, from his performance he will definitely know how to adjust the time plan. If his performance is low, he will definitely want to improve. He will need to change time plans. If he continues to change it in this manner, before his third year he must have being able to understand the system; his lecture time, his reading time and examination time. So his plans at this stage will be effective and maturity will be attained. His efficiency will increase with better performance. When plans are effective, over a process or duration of time, its application becomes a routine or principal.

EFFECTIVE MONITORING OF PROCESS

Monitoring of process is just a way of staying smart throughout the process. Gathering information about functions and operation of the process, this will enable you quick analysis of the system and proffer how best you can function or operate to attain maximum result. Monitoring of a process becomes effective when you are fully in control. It means you surpass all odds, to take charge to direct the system for long time success.

Actions are best managed when they are being monitored and worked on. Every individual are responsible for their actions whether good or bad. This is a more reasons why actions should be monitored for effective outcome. For you to achieve your goal you need to be discipline, which will enable you for effective monitoring of the process. When you discipline yourself, you accept rules and condition to function maximally.

Process monitoring is having sufficient information about a system, its functions and operations all through the required time. Effective monitoring is when your continuous process monitoring have yielded things like; growth in overall performance, increase in processing speed, efficiency in process, more refined and better quality etcetera. Before you can effectively monitor a process be smart to study the system as it changes and how it can increase or reduce production outcome. In a seed planted for example; the farmer water's it, he may not be very sure when to water it at evening or the proper timing. I know if he does water the grains as they grow at odd times they may die or weaken, once he observed the plants are being affected negatively, he will immediately stop and change timing. He gets to a level when he already knows when and how to do everything to help the plant produce a better yield. That stage is called maturity stage. It's as a result of his effectively monitoring how the grains respond to the season and climate.

Maturity gives you an awareness to deploy resources for effective process monitoring. Monitoring of process cannot be effective if there is no step by step approach to study the operation and functions of the system. Effective monitoring leads to efficiency of process and improvement in processing. Monitoring of process gives you the sense of responsibility that switches on your positive thought for better strategy to achieve better result.

EFFECTIVE GROWTH MONITORING

When growth is being monitored? It becomes more challenging to go less than the previous result. Monitoring of growth challenges you to apply more skills, more strength, more strategy and more discipline into the system to always produce better result. Growth becomes effective when its visibility is recommendable. This can be achieved by constant monitoring of growth. Effective monitoring begins with; monitoring the elements of growth, nature of growth, the environment and season. To always improve or increase growth monitoring need to be effective in order to attain maturity. Without effective monitoring; growth could possibly decrease or reduce after the first increase in growth. That is why is necessary to have your eyes on the process and understand every element and function of the operations.

To ensure constant growth in a process; life, career or organisation, there must be effective monitoring of growth. After every first victory people wait for the next victory, but when it never comes they assume your first victory was luck. You become successful with series of victories. Though every life has its challenges but it takes determinations and discipline to remain focus when all you can see is weakness. Maturity is being able to effectively study the growth over some period of time and you now able to make best decision on best procedure for excellent output. Considering the University student that have to change his time plans to function better, can still be object to growth monitoring. If his result; after first year increases semester after semester. He can put in mind those elements that have enabled the constant growth to ensure continuous increase in CGP. For him to come out with flying colours he needs to monitor his results or growth effectively; his score in each course, the course credit load, year after year.

Monitoring of growth energizes someone for better performance. When growth are being monitored the mind is being put into work, thoughts that will bring about better performance will begin to crop up from the mind. Great strategy for better performance emanate from effective growth monitoring. It's very difficult to have continuous growth without effective monitoring of the elements of growth. No matter how gifted or talented, you have to monitor growth to always have improved result. Monitoring gives the sense of re-strategising and re-organising when challenges confront the system. After learning from the challenge and you resolve it, you begin to enjoy consistent growth. This period when growth is consistent is your maturity stage.

Maturity stage is when you have full understanding about the process and how to make growth efficient. When you know what to do, how to do it, when to do it and how to sustain it, you are said to be matured. Growth doesn't come easy, it requires a lot of learning or training, endurance and discipline, Continuous learning on the process always guarantee growth. Only effective monitoring of growth can keep you going with better performance. If a bird stops swinging his wings, it stop going higher. Nothing gets better on its own. Effort must be applied to make a motion. Things don't get better until they are made better. The more swings the bird makes the higher it fly. Just as the student the more commitment he shows in monitoring his growth and his plans, the better his outcome and growth in his CGP.

CHAPTER 6

REPRODUCTION OF NEW GRAINS

Trees produce seeds in a fruit, but until the fruit is let out of the tree it can't become another tree

Reproduction is a process of giving birth or re-creating of new species; as same as the original or better and more refined ones. Reproduction is a proof of maturity. It is the easiest way to know when a life or process has gotten to its matured stage. In life when someone is used to a skill in a system, studies, career or routine, he is said to have mastered the function of the system. For reproduction to take place maturity have to be in place, just as with seed so it's human skills and talents.

You have to be very good, to be very impactful. Like someone that went for training on a particular course or operation in a company, or for self; if he give it all attention during training and learn all that is required and become very good. He will definitely be very good in impacting the knowledge gain. You can't give what you don't have. Every seed that grow well produce good fruits, their yields are always great. So, in any endeavour ensure you are growing well. Get on the ladder up and never look down until you found comfort on the top most top. The only way to prove you are a master in anything is the ability to create and recreate it; to make its own very kind with more improved qualities. Mastery is the height of maturity. Every plants is expected to reproduce at maturity, reproduction is essential stage of plant circle. The better the growth stage, the better the harvest or reproduced seed. The reproductive stage earns the seed satisfaction and credibility, same it does to man. If after a growth process, like graduating from a course or institution; you are unable to impact in the society. Your satisfaction is not met and your credibility not tested.

Maturity and reproductive stage are close stages, inbuilt together with slim boundary. Immediately a seed get matured, just same time reproduction stage begins. Same is expected for human. But human out of inability to follow law, they chose knowledge of craft. For everything made to obey natural laws, they all do so except human; like fish needs water, seed needs soil, Birds needs space to fly, human needs God. But often times, only human fall out of law of nature. We think God want us, God had always needed us to direct us, yet we need him more because that his direction is the best way to go. There is no better way that can guarantee such a wonderful harvest without God. Only he does it marvellously. Without the soil seed, can't think of germination. Seeds don't grow in tiles; fish don't survive in land, so men don't get their grains of potential to maturity without God to direct the process. Seek God in all you do along the process, within the time and ever then after. God is all waiting to take charge, give him control of you. All you need is acknowledge him in your life as your lord and saviour in all you do.

To be impactful, you should have sufficient knowledge of the subject. Knowledge is wisdom in application, where the mastery of the subject in question leads to efficient maturity stage. This kind of maturity you are rest assure of good reproduction. For you to master a skill you must be very good in impacting the same skill. Seeds with better yield produce better harvest. That one reason you must keep improving your skills. This impartation always earns satisfaction if you chose to train other individuals who will walk on your path. Through satisfaction of oneself comes with the realisation of our true grains of potential and destiny. Our tree begins to make trees, if we allow our fruits to benefit others. Only then they can help us to plant it where they can grow and bear more fruits. One could gain progress in life over a period of time, but until you give out, your seeds can't be planted, for more trees to grow. The seed you produced is your new tree, the more you give out the seeds produced, the more you are planting. You need more trees to have shade. One tree doesn't form the best shade.

Every man has the ability to create and make changes in anything, but he should have adequate knowledge to do so, he acquires knowledge and ready to make it happen. In the process he needs persons to work with even when he knows what to do; assistant is often needed to grow well. He will impact his knowledge on the people working with him, explain to them the direction he want to sail the ship. So through this impartation, reproduction of that which he has conceived will be given birth to. Before you become anything, your thought must have begun to frequent that for some time through your subconscious mind.

Without the view of reproduction maturity is of no essence. Same goes to human; without the aim of impartation, knowledge is useless. If what you know is not helping anyone to grow, then you are not producing fruits. Remember reproduction begins immediately during maturity, so once you master that skill impact on others. Don't hide knowledge; it can only limit your growth. Great men don't grow on themselves alone. They grow on others as well. Let's consider some tips that can help us in reproduction or impartation;

CREATING THE RIGHT ENVIRONMENT

For reproduction to take place in Plant, The grains have to be pollinated; either by animals, wind or insects. Just as Ovulation period in animals before gestation. Even in our profession, career and trainings same thing happens. Before you can impact Knowledge on someone, he must be ready for impartation. You must also be willing; the environment must give room for the learning process if you both are ready.

Other enabling factors, that could boost the learning process will come from the setting; classroom, laboratory or conference room Etcetera. How conducive your environment is can boost your concentration and enhance your skills.

Your resource materials can also make knowledge easily accessible. All this put in place is the environment you creating to ensure effect impartation of knowledge. The quality of resource materials, the nature of classroom, coaching ability; all will have great impact on the seed you produce at the end of the training.

Environment affects the quality of seed, just as the nature of the parents' seed also affects the new seed. You train to impact and make better than previous quality, because inventions and growth have set competitors globally in all works of life through technology on quality of products. To make your Seeds great and better, there should be improved training skills you could adopt to ensure they get better than you had.

When organisation is set to recruit new staffs for instance, they create avenue for training of new staffs. This will enable proper integration of the new staffs into the organisation system, rules and operations. During the training exercise new staffs are exposed to some of the company materials like; tools, their objective and vision. These are to prepare the new staff against the task ahead and follow every step by step on the training.

After this induction training stage the new staffs must have acquired some knowledge in line with their job descriptions. The quality of resources (both human and material) at their disposer during the training, will determine how reflective the training will be to their various departments or job functions. So it's very necessary to make good preparation when the need to impact or training new staffs arises. Creating good learning environment is one basic step to impactful training.

Training can't be every time, it has to be scheduled. Plants don't produce all season, even animal don't give birth always. It is very essential you make appropriate arrangement for good training time and period. It will determine the quality of staffs and personnel's in the company.

CREATE THE MOMENTUM TO INFLUENCE

Influence comes as a result of impartation on once life. Momentum is your willingness to impact on others. Your eagerness to impact the knowledge and your composer will earn you the influence. So, you have to create such momentum before you can effectively influence them to follow your teaching. Remember you can't give what you don't have. So, you must read and practice also. Mastery comes through a long period of practice. Practice can never be too much, because it makes skills better. Your willingness to influence will enable you good preparation and research. The influence you gain over your subject is limitless, when you really impactful. Willpower will always withstand every challenge you may encounter in the process. If you acquired adequate knowledge during training, then creating that momentum to influence motivates you naturally as well and enables effective learning, likability and familiarity.

SEE VALUE IN YOURSELF

Self appreciation is confident that every person that interacts often with others needs. It creates a big picture of you before your imagination and it reflect in the way you carry yourself. Self value makes you believe that you know what to do and how to do it. If you know what to teach and you are not confident, you can't impact it, so it as same as you don't know it. You can't teach nor can you impact. Teaching or impacting comes from overloads of acquired knowledge. If you have too much, you give too much. That is value for teaching quality. You must have it to teach it. Confident of oneself goes a long way to make excellent class. The trainee and the trainer enjoy real class learning scenario; where question and answer will be addressed, well explained with illustrations and demonstrations.

You must have value in order to give value to others. Impacting on others is giving value to them. Showing them the structures to enhance their knowledge and become more productive. You must have good knowledge of the subject, before you can impact properly.

Some years back during my Industrial training (Tertiary industrial intermediary attachment training), before my graduation year. It was a six months duration period. Students are allowed to look out for a place of attachment for them. Lucky enough i found a place, to acquire the knowledge and experience for the program.

The resumption day, i was giving a voluminous textbook, with a lot of different program syntax to memories within two weeks. After the first two weeks i could not get everything right, so another two weeks was given. After which i was given a class of cooperate student from financial organisation to trained on those syntax. At first i felt like; during their introduction, these guys got a lot working for them, family, degrees and good job. But at a level i said to myself, you are the trainer here, if they know better they wouldn't be in this class. So i am the only person that knows what i want to teach. I echo in my heart "you listen let me show you how". I begin the class with the value i was able to generate within me that i am to impact on them, not the other way round. I took them through some weeks training.

And after the class, they were like can you take us on private coaching. Some of them made such demand, yet they never knew i was only student for an industrial training attachment. That because i saw value in myself, willing to impact the knowledge gained after i had read the textbook and with a lot of hands on system practical's, i developed confident in myself. When you see value in yourself you generate internal confident that builds your ability to attain. Preparedness gives awareness of self value and confident. If you are prepared yourself value is always high, your confident is high, you have the 'i can do it mentality'.

Before you can impact knowledge on others you must see yourself capable of impacting that knowledge. Self image, boost self value and self value gives confident. Confident is the courage to conquer, which builds your self esteem. Self value is very important in impartation. It creates the arena for discipline and control, that the training or impartation needed mainly to be awesome.

GIVE AND SHOW GRATITUDE

Gratitude is the expression of thanks or appreciation. It's the feelings of being grateful. This feeling gives satisfaction and contentment. Once you can develop it, impacting knowledge will be very easy. Not everything we do we expect financial reward or instant reward; mostly in training or learning the trainer must not have financial gain as a motivating factor, if he does it will not be gratifying enough to motivate him to impact.

People that are never contented can never impact positively. Contentment boosts the feeling of gratitude, whether to God or to humanity. If you are not gratifying enough, you may be carried away by your pride. Feeling of pride is a distraction in a learning environment, either from the instructor or student. The feeling of gratitude subdues pride and arrogance, thereby create satisfaction.

Appreciating trainee performance from trainer goes a long way to motivate and stir up the entire class to put in more effort to learn. Also trainee can encourage trainer with appreciative words and humility, it builds that connection between the trainer and the trainee. This connection provides room for better understanding with good practical illustrations. To reproduce your seed, you must learn how to appreciate and show appreciation to your trainee or your trainers.

SHOW LOVE AND SEEK UNDERSTAND

When you genuinely love someone, you will be ever willing to impact knowledge on that person. This a natural thing, which is to say; with this understand between you as the trainer to your trainee, you both knows the limit of your relationship is to foster understanding in the learning arena. When you often appreciate them and encourage them to learn both in practicals and theory. Soon your influence will begin to affect them positively.

The knowledge you are impacting can better be understood in love and tolerance. Good teacher to student relationship makes learning arena friendly and tension free. It's necessary you show love to those you are impacting knowledge on. It makes the learning environment friendly and accommodating. That class is friendly doesn't mean that the class will not be run on disciplinary rules. With more integrity and love, learning is more gainful. Love reduces tension.

Students naturally are always scared when they see you know far more than them. Mostly when you are their teacher, so showing them love is a way to draw them closer and you give them room to relax their mind and learn. Once you can make the relationship mutual with understanding, the students are free to express themselves, ask questions and make contributions.

When you show people love is like you welcome them to yourself and they become more open to you; then they will become more open to learn no matter how challenging the environment or course of study.

The knowledge or training that will impact positively on a life or person is done with great understanding and love, you can only understand someone that is open to you. People only become open when they are shown love or experience love.

CHAPTER 7

ACTUALISATION OF PURPOSE

Harvest attracts many; the planter, the buyer and the seller ensure not to be carried away

This is the point where you feel accomplished. You have arrived at your purpose. Your goals are met. This is that point where your efforts throughout the process begin to benefit you. Your results are speaking for you. Those you trained are grown about training others. The outcome is bringing you fame; more friends and contact. Everybody wants to associate with you. You are a success story. When you get to your purpose, these are the common signs; you begin to reconnect with old friends, become influential. People will want to reckon with you. You receive pleasantries from different works of life, awards and appreciation for job well done.

Actualisation of purpose comes with rewards and influence. People naturally begin to like you and follow your ways. You become a man of influence, someone others seek after. You become master to many and a source of inspiration and a mentor. You become a point of reference people will seek after.

Accomplishment comes when you are fully manifesting in your purpose and potentials. What you need here mostly is; A little rest, thought rest is not really much advisable for longer than required but a little will do. It's just like a little self reward for the work well done. A little celebration, what is all the hard times for if you can't enjoy your accomplishment. You deserve to celebrate your victory and accomplishment of purpose. Treat yourself nicely, call some close friends, business associates, colleague or partner, eat out, party etc. This will create that sense of fulfilment in you, the celebrations and the satisfaction from the accomplishment of your purpose will boost you to another new height. You're thought of what next to accomplish and what next to do will become the recent thought in your mind.

At this stage there are attribute you must keep constant to ensure your grains of potentials stay fresh and always anew. This will make it constantly useful not just only to you but to others as well. Like listed below, you should have attributes inclusive of the below list;

1. Constant quest for knowledge
2. Good family relationship and relationship with others
3. Be part of a team
4. Travel more to see more
5. Learn more new things